GOLF
IS A
GOOD WALK
SPOILED

GOLF
IS A
GOOD WALK
SPOILED

GEORGE EBERL

Foreword by C. Grant Spaeth

TAYLOR PUBLISHING COMPANY
DALLAS, TEXAS

Copyright © 1992 by George Eberl

Published by Taylor Publishing Company
          1550 West Mockingbird Lane
          Dallas, Texas 75235

Designed by Deborah Jackson-Jones

Library of Congress Cataloging-in-Publication Data

Eberl, George.
    Golf is a good walk spoiled / George Eberl : foreword by
  C. Grant Spaeth.
      p.   cm.
    ISBN 0-87833-791-1 : $15.95
    1. Golf—Humor.   2. Golf—Rules—Humor.   I. Title.
  GV967.E24   1992
  796.352'0207—dc20   91-43044
                                                              CIP

Printed in the United States of America
10 9 8 7 6 5 4 3 2

To the memory of P.J. Boatwright, Jr.,
whose passion for golf and its rules was contagious

ACKNOWLEDGMENTS

For the most part, writing a book is a
lonely business, yet in the final analysis,
it isn't done alone. Others have a hand
in it, for reasons inspirational or
practical, subtle or apparent. My
cap is doffed to Rhonda Glenn,
for her unflagging enthusiasm and
encouragement and her entrepreneurial
skills; to Grant Spaeth, for his great
good cheer and the steady push on me
to stick with it; to Bob Sommers, who,
with Frank "Sandy" Tatum, hired me in
the first place, thus placing me in the
position to write this book; and to the
Orrs and the Curries, in Scotland, who
with other friends in that grand land
supplied so much of the raw and
precious material. And a special word
for Jeff Hall, the USGA's young Rules
maven, who read the manuscript and
steered me around any fatal gaffes.
Thank you, all of you.

CONTENTS

FOREWORD

In the chapter of this book entitled "Hazards to Your Health," the author describes a memorable incident that occurred during a 1984 tournament at the Atlanta Athletic Club in Duluth, Georgia. It involved two golfers, David Jacobsen and Mike Podolak, and a large body of water at the eighteenth hole, and it decided the U.S. Mid-Amateur Championship that year.

That championship had special meaning for me; I was Secretary of the USGA at the time, and Chairman of the championship. Having served often as a referee, I was aware of the unpredictable turns possible in these tournaments. As it happened, events kept officials busy making decisions in the Mid-Amateur, and appropriately, the USGA reporter covering the tournament for the organizations's magazine, *Golf Journal*, would later focus his story on the many bizarre incidents giving that Mid-Amateur its distinctive flavor.

The writer was George Eberl, and as he and I had done during earlier USGA championships, and would do in later competitions, we indulged ourselves in endless what-ifs. What if David Jacobsen had done this, or Mike Podolak had done that? Multiply it many times and you have enough material for a book.

And here it is. Not all incidents in golf lead to Decisions based on the Rules of Golf, but many do, and those of us who spend a fair amount of our summer days playing golf official must know the Rules and Decisions, and certainly where to find those that are applicable. Sadly enough, even that isn't foolproof; just about the time you are convinced nothing new is possible, you learn that it just isn't so.

New Decisions in golf must often be spanked into life when absolutely unique occurrences take place; that, in large part, is what this book is all about. It is also about golf's existing Rules and Decisions and how they have been put to the test over the years under varying conditions and in myriad locales.

It is somehow reassuring to know that whether you are playing golf in America, or in Scotland, or in South Africa, or India, those Rules and Decisions remain constant save, perhaps, for a free lift from a hippopotamus hoofprint, or relief from an irritable cobra that has developed an untoward fondness for your golf ball.

If I were to single out a central theme that has always been high in my own consciousness about golf and its Rules and Decisions, it is this: the story of those Rules and their resultant Decisions reflect the fundamental humanity of the sport. It may seem fashionable to mock golf's Rules, contending that they're stuffy and often incomprehensible, a grammatical jungle; the Decisions are usually spared such criticism, largely, I suspect, because they somehow introduce flesh and blood to the matter-of-fact realm of the Rules. Rules govern golfers; Decisions *are* golfers.

I can't shake the feeling that this is a book that needed to be written, if for no other reason than to remind all of us that golf is not only a game with a long and often humorous tradition, but also a game that in its way is a microcosm of this world in which we live—a game rich in humanity.

Mark Twain may have believed that golf is a good walk spoiled, but I would like to think this book will make that walk more tolerable.

—C. GRANT SPAETH
President, United States Golf Association

Golf is a good walk spoiled.

—MARK TWAIN

INTRODUCTION: GOLF IS FLOG BACKWARDS

One of the charms of golf is its own sense of tradition, and perhaps this tradition is nowhere more prominently on display than in its regulations. I avoid the term *Rules*, because the Rules, while useful, tend to be extraordinarily dull, for the most part deserving little serious attention beyond what you need to know to play the game fairly and enjoyably.

If the Rules are a necessary evil within golf, it should be pointed out that these dismal, legalistic, profoundly uninteresting blemishes on the game are also the basis for the *Decisions*, which are often fascinating.

Essentially, here's what happens. You and I go out to play golf by the Rules (and each of us carries one of those little Rules books to help us do so); likely as not during our rounds, something occurs that is not covered by the Rules. At least, we can't find reasonable explanations in our 132-page booklets. We have these options later, after we've muddled through our round: we may dig through the compact 471-page book of Decisions to see if the same experience has been had by someone ahead of us and was subsequently resolved by the priesthood of Rules experts; or we may call or write to either of the game's governing bodies, the United States Golf Association on this side of the Atlantic Ocean, or the Royal and Ancient Golf Club of St. Andrews, Scotland, in charge of decision making for most of the rest of the world.

In fact, that distinction isn't quite true any longer; the USGA and the R&A used to be somewhat independent in their decision-making functions, but now they consult each other and, in conjunction, annually release new Decisions based on the Rules of Golf, a batch of Decisions that bears the names of both of the two approving bodies.

Carry this sequence one step further, however; what actually happens on the golf course creates the need for Decisions based on the Rules of Golf. The ultimate delight lies within what happens. This is where the fun begins.

For example, the Rules cover a category called "outside agencies," which might include everything from dogs in transit, to a referee, or marker, or a child passing the course on a bicycle—anything other than wind and water and things that belong to an affected player's side. The Rules are quite clear on matters concerning outside agencies; if a dog runs off with your ball after it has come to rest, you replace your ball as near as possible to the point where the dog picked it up. Reasonable enough.

Now let us suppose this outside agency isn't something as innocent as a pesky dog; instead, it is a rattlesnake in a bunker. It is next to your ball, and it is visibly irritable. Must you play your shot where it lies? The Rules had taken little account of poisonous snakes until 1967. They weren't a problem in Scotland.

In that year, this unpleasant reality was brought to the USGA's attention after a match played by two women in Florida—and herein lies the entertaining facet of Rules and Decisions. In the rattlesnake instance, the ball's owner wanted some relief; her opponent was not in a generous mood, allowing only that she would ward off any thrusts by the snake with her nine-iron while the ball's owner should attempt her shot in their match.

The ball's owner confessed she would have liked to wrap the nine-iron around her opponent's neck.

Belatedly, sweet reason prevailed; the USGA asserted that the game wasn't intended to threaten life or limb, so the player whose ball rested near the reptile should have been allowed to drop another ball in a similar setting (minus snake, of course) but no closer to the hole. This logic was extended as well to wasps, red ants, and other menacing creatures.

There you are: zany incidents that are tied directly or indirectly to Decisions based on the Rules of Golf, occasionally, perhaps, helping to create a new Decision (the rattlesnake in the bunker was one such instance). The Rule may fascinate no one, but a rattlesnake will certainly waken the most apathetic and indifferent of souls.

These happenings often have outlived the matches or tournaments in which they occurred. Few who have heard the story about the shot to the green that rolled under the skirt of a spectator seated at greenside will forget the incident, although they may be hard pressed to remember the tournament (The Masters) or the player who hit the ball (Gene Sarazen).

Codified Rules came into being in the mid-1700s, in Scotland, and at the outset included only thirteen Rules, far from the thirty-four that fill much of today's little book.

In the interest of linguistic precision, the Rules often succeed sadly in being all but impenetrable. In 1982, when I worked as managing editor for *Golf Journal*, the USGA's official magazine, I was approached one afternoon by John Morris, then USGA director of communications. He asked me to convert a particular passage from the Rules into understandable prose.

I spent a couple hours in this translation chore, passing the finished product to Morris. He carried it to Harry Easterly, then the USGA's senior executive director, who, in turn, offered it to the late P. J. Boatwright Jr., perhaps this country's ultimate authority on the Rules of Golf. A few weeks of silence ensued before Morris dropped by one day with the reaction. As it turned out, what I had written was wrong; it was not what the Rule said, or at least not what it had intended to say.

It could be argued that I should have been ashamed of myself. After all, I worked at Golf House, the USGA headquarters, and I did edit its official magazine. Turn that around, however; even I, a professional editor who worked for the USGA, could not understand what the Rules writers were trying to say. How easy is it for those players around America who can't simply walk down the hall and ask an expert?

It is this incomprehensibility that has created more heated clubhouse discussions and, too often, arguments won by debaters capable of generating more heat than light.

It has served, of course, to create this priesthood of Rules mavens, and they may be found each late winter and spring conducting expensive Rules seminars around America, usually under the careful eye of the USGA or the PGA, which has a powerful interest in a clear understanding of the Rules. Frequently, the PGA, LPGA, and PGA Senior Tour officials are seen handing out rulings on national television, and, surprisingly, they are rendering decisions for professionals who often know little of the Rules by which they play the game.

An odd statistic surfaced a few years back when it was found that something like six of the PGA's hundreds of Tour players subscribed to the annual Decisions-update service. At the time, it cost $25. Compare this with the amount of money they would receive for finishing even sixtieth in a tournament.

A penalty stroke or two could cost thousands of dollars.

These Decisions are one of the tools of their well-paying trade. It would be tantamount in one sense to a doctor persisting in the use of leeches, not keeping up on the latest medical findings; although in this more innocent situation, golfers are hurting only themselves.

Craig Stadler, for example, found out the hard way—twice in 1987—when he failed to keep up with the Rules and Decisions, a failing he ruefully admitted to after the fact.

In the better-known Stadler malfeasance, he was viewed on nationwide TV during the San Diego Open placing a towel on the wet ground under a pine tree to protect his trousers. His ball had rolled under the tree, and he was forced to make his escape shot on his knees. Unrealized by him—and it was a Decision that was part of the latest booklet published for 1987—he was building a stance. It was a situation born of an incident in 1982 at Pinehurst during the NCAA Championship; the USGA and Royal and Ancient agreed that the player had built a stance with his towel.

9

You or I may argue the logic of that Decision, but if I'm playing golf for many thousands of dollars, it behooves me to know such a Decision exists. In the Stadler case, the irony was this: a viewer saw it in a TV highlight the next day and telephoned PGA officials. Technically, Craig had turned in an incorrect scorecard, ground for disqualification. And that's what happened.

He was nailed again during the British Open when he lifted an embedded ball in the rough, a breach of Rule 25-2. It cost him, and after this second disaster of the year, he was moved to comment, "I had better learn the Rules." And the Decisions.

Quite incidentally, one thing you should never do is present a USGA or an R&A Rules specialist with a hypothetical case. Boatwright, for example, was outspoken about this; he would not be drawn into speculative cases, the "what-if" sort of thing. If something happened, Boatwright was unstinting in his patience and attention; if it was something you dreamed up, he wouldn't offer a ruling, hypothetical or otherwise.

It is useful to players everywhere that the USGA and the Royal and Ancient have gotten their

10

acts literally together. In the past, something might receive one ruling in America and another in Great Britain. A classic case occurred in the 1974 English Open Amateur Stroke Play Championship, at Moortown, when Nigel Denham, from Yorkshire County, had his adrenalin flowing as he approached the eighteenth green, directly behind the Moortown clubhouse (the club's identity was not offered in the Royal and Ancient Decisions book's report).

Pumped up, he stroked his iron shot well over the green. The ball struck a path, took a long bounce up some steps, and rolled directly through an open door and into the clubhouse. The clubhouse was not out of bounds at the time.

Denham followed his ball into the clubhouse. Apparently, it had deflected off a wall and found its way into the bar area, coming to rest under a table. The setting had a preciousness of its own; here is a player, lying two in the bar, facing a difficult shot in the presence of a crowd of drinking competitors lined up at the clubhouse bar, some of whom might be celebrating, while others would rather forget.

The player moved the table and surrounding chairs and sized up his shot. To his surprise, he was able to see the flag of the eighteenth hole through a

11

window. It would require an exacting shot, but stranger things had happened, he was sure.

He walked over and opened the window, returned to his ball, and after a few practice swings, gently lined his shot through the open window. It rolled onto the green and came to rest about twelve feet from the hole. Even his barside adversaries were forced to compliment him.

He concluded this remarkable performance by making the putt for an extraordinary par.

Word of the incident got back to the tournament committee, but since everything seemed within the Rules, his par on the eighteenth was accepted (no, he did not win the tournament). However, unsure about the propriety of some of the actions in the clubhouse, the committee wrote to the Royal and Ancient, reporting the details.

Some time went by, of course, but at last the R&A responded. The committee was told that the player was perfectly correct to enter the clubhouse for his ball if it was not deemed out of bounds, and, moreover, he was correct to move the tables and chairs, all movable objects. Opening the window, however, was improper; it improved the line of play, and as the clubhouse was an immovable obstruction and the window was part of the clubhouse, that should have earned a penalty. Nevertheless, the committee's decision at the time prevailed.

During the many long sessions involving the USGA and R&A Rules experts that led to the 1984 consolidation of the Rules and Decisions by the two organizations, many differences of opinion surfaced, and this incident inspired one of those differences. While the R&A and USGA agreed that the club-house should have been out of bounds in the first place, the USGA argued persuasively that the win-dow should have been regarded as movable, and not a line-of-play factor, thus opposing the R&A's posi-tion. The R&A accepted the USGA contention.

The willingness of the two ruling bodies to unite themselves in this amalgamation of the Rules of Golf involved an element of give and take. They had not always agreed, but they were willing to bend.

A final prefatory note: this is not intended as a book about the Rules. Rather, it is a recital of the more novel, comic, or dramatic incidents on golf courses, some of which have induced golf's legislators to interpret, alter, or expand the regulations govern-ing play of the game. It is also intended as a collecting point for related commentary that has been inspired by these incidents and by the game itself.

Indeed, golf is an irresistible subject for anyone inclined to generate opinions at the flip of a golf tee. So you will find views and incidents quite separate from Decisions and Rules, but, we trust, both relevant and germane to the game. If other little tidbits of information that have some trivia merit sneak into the text, all the better.

The Rules are always there, lingering in the background, an unavoidable reality. Mercifully, however, golf is still a game played by people.

Oddly enough, occasional Decisions have been rendered that only indirectly involved what happened on the golf course. Among the more memorable instances of this was the case in England of an amateur tournament co-sponsored by a bank and an insurance company. The life insurance firm wanted to reward the champion of this event with one year's free premium on a life insurance policy.

Quite correctly, however, the company did not want to jeopardize the player's amateur status, so it took pains to question the Royal and Ancient on the propriety of the proposal. The R&A shared the inquiry with its cousin across the seas, the USGA, and after an appropriate, thoughtful delay, a judgment emerged from the Royal and Ancient headquarters, housed in that awesome blockhouse of a building behind the first tee of the Old Course in St. Andrews. (And no, the Old Course does not belong to the Royal and Ancient despite the proximity; it belongs to the city of St. Andrews. This is a mistake made with painful frequency in this country, even in magazines that should know better. One wrote breathlessly of the exclusivity of membership in the St. Andrews Golf Club, whose Old Course was one of the more chi-chi in all of Great Britain. Exclusive it isn't.)

Meanwhile, back at the insurance company's inquiry—although it hasn't been confirmed, there's a suspicion that Frank Hannigan, a USGA official known for both his Rules expertise and his sense of humor, was lurking in the background when the Decision was handed down:

It would be acceptable for the insurance company to offer a year's free premium to the winner of the amateur tournament; however, if the player should die during the course of the premium period, any payment by the insurance company to a beneficiary would cost the deceased his amateur status.

15

I

ANIMALS: OF FEATHERS AND FUR. . . .

If a ball comes to rest in dangerous proximity to a hippopotamus or crocodile, another ball may be dropped at a safe distance, no nearer the hole, without penalty.

—LOCAL RULE, NYANZA CLUB, BRITISH EAST AFRICA, 1950

17

During a Rules seminar in the early 1980s at the Plainfield Country Club in Plainfield, New Jersey, a student attending the seminar from the Philippines brought up a problem the Scots would never have faced. Cobras liked to hang around the tangled roots of banyan trees, a breed of East Indian fig whose adventitious roots growing out of overhead branches exercise a potentially fatal attraction for stray golf balls. What are your options if you discover your golf ball dangerously close to a cobra?

It is not surprising that animals occupy a generous niche in the Decisions book; not only is golf played out of doors, but also golf courses have much to recommend them for beasts that aren't especially fond of housing developments and shopping malls.

The section of the world or of the country determines the character of the animal population, of course. For example, in most parts of the world it isn't necessary to have a Local Rule to permit the free lift of one's golf ball from the hoofprint of a hippopotamus. Zambia and Jinja, Uganda, however, endure heavy rains at certain times of the year, and hippos aren't featherweights, so when they tromp over the waterlogged landscape, you know they've been there.

Indeed, the Scots had little animal life other than pets and random livestock, notably sheep, to consider in their earliest Rules. Burrowing animals gradually showed up in the Decisions, and ball thieves among the furry and feathered populations made their appearances in golf's legislative documents when they became a nuisance to players.

Cobras were a special case, and they fell into the same category as that Florida rattlesnake in 1967. Here are the question and answer from that instance, also applicable to the cobra inquiry:

Q: In a women's team match a player's ball came to rest in a bunker beside a green. As the player entered the bunker to play the shot, she observed a rattlesnake on the sand a short distance from her ball.

Her opponent insisted that she must play the ball since she was not permitted to touch or move a loose impediment in a hazard. She offered generously to stand guard with her nine-iron in case the snake attacked.

"Does the definition of 'loose impediments', which stipulates 'worms and insects', include rattlesnakes? Or would it be better to forfeit the hole and use the wedge on the opponent?" the affected player inquired. If she had killed the snake, her opponent might have claimed she was testing the consistency of the sand.

A: It is not reasonable to expect a player to play from such a dangerous situation, and the Rules do not so intend. In equity (fairness) the player should have been allowed to place a ball in the hazard, or in a similar nearby hazard, in a situation she did not regard as dangerous, as near as possible to the spot where the ball lay and in a lie similar to that which it originally occupied.

The same procedure would be permissible had the ball lain through the green.

Attention is called to Rule 32-3 (now Rule 25-1b) giving relief from a hole, cast, or runway made by a reptile.

A snake is not a loose impediment within the meaning of Definition 17. It is an outside agency under Definition 22.

21

When this Decision was made in 1967, it covered an assortment of dangers ranging from red ants to alligators. Cobras could be added reasonably to the list of dangerous creatures.

A Local Rule at the Glen Canyon course in Arizona spares players uncomfortable moments: "If your ball lands within a club's length of a rattlesnake you are allowed to move the ball." Measuring that club length, of course, could be nerve wracking.

Precedents did exist, however, for the rattlesnake finding. A ruling similar to that in the rattlesnake incident was made during the 1949 United States Amateur Championship, at the Oak Hill Country Club in Rochester, New York. A bunker infested by yellow jackets prompted officials to grant relief to players, allowing each to place a ball in a similar setting no closer to the hole.

On the other hand, if the poor creature dies, its golf status changes dramatically. For example, Decision 23/6 decrees that "a dead land crab is a natural object and thus a loose impediment and not an obstruction." Removal of the crab (found in a bunker) is not allowed, as it would be a breach of Rule 13-4.

But a variation on the dead-animal theme occurred in October 1987 during the first U.S.

Women's Mid-Amateur Championship, played at Southern Hills Country Club in Tulsa, Oklahoma. A player's ball came to rest against a dead squirrel. Officials allowed the player to drop another ball a short distance away and no closer to the hole. Aside from the mess that might have been created with any attempt to strike the ball, there was a secondary fear that the dead rodent may have been diseased.

Considerations of danger have not always brought kindly legislation. The story is told of a stroke-play competition in the Far East in which two players on the final nine holes arrived at a teeing area where they discovered some water buffalo placidly grazing. The beasts glanced at the players with bleak and suspicious eyes.

The players, properly apprehensive, decided to forego that tee area and headed for the forward tees, from where they played, far removed from the buffalo. Upon their return to the clubhouse when their rounds were completed, the two men turned in their scorecards to the committee and amiably reported the incident with the animals.

To their astonishment, they were disqualified from the tournament for playing from outside the teeing ground and not correcting their error before

23

playing from the next teeing ground, or, if it was the final hole of the round, before leaving the putting green.

Not all cautious players are treated so harshly by Rules committees. Four players were golfing at Brora, in Scotland's Sutherland County, when at the seventeenth green, they watched a cow giving birth to twin calves between the markers of the eighteenth tee. Out of deference to the laboring mother, they decided to tee off from a point comfortably in front of the usual eighteenth tee. Later, they applied for a ruling from the Royal and Ancient, eliciting the reply that while their action had broken a rule technically, their deed was within the spirit of the game, and no penalty should be levied. The Secretary of the R&A's Rules Committee also inquired about the condition of the mother cow, expressing the hope that she and her twins were doing well.

It seems to suggest that menacing buffalo are not grounds for prudence, but cows in the throes of birth are another matter.

The story is told, too, about Nick Price during a round in South Africa. As he was about to hit off the tee, a herd of boar charged across the fairway a couple of hundred yards in front of him. Price, understandably unnerved, flinched, raising up slightly, and hit a low shot directly at the racing animals.

As fates would have it, his ball struck the rear end of one of the beasts, lodging in a most indelicate location. Needless to say, this hastened the boar's pace, and Price's golf ball was long gone.

Under the outside agency Decision, he was allowed a free drop at the point where his ball and the unfortunate boar had converged.

Much of the fussing about animals falls within their identity as "outside agencies," something of a limbo for the creatures, and not very enlightening from the standpoint of the players.

For example, how would you like to be one of the sheep at the Pitlochry course in central Scotland that sees to it the course is neatly trimmed on a daily basis, including the banks around the bunkers, only to be regarded somewhat impersonally as an outside agency?

For that matter, to exaggerate the case of the dead crab above, and another Decision offering the same judgment about a dead rat (loose impediment), a dead elephant in a bunker may not be moved (it would take some moving in any case), but you would be allowed relief from a *live* one under its outside-agency status. Outside the bunker, you could theoretically shove a dead elephant aside, and you could claim relief from a live one under the equity ruling covering danger.

Indeed, a sign that recurs at various points in Africa reads, "Elephants Have the Right of Way." Another common sign: "You Are in Wild Animal Country." This has to be dissuasive for the player who is not foolhardy.

The attack motif is not limited, of course, to wild animals; two players at the Dungannon Golf Links in Ireland were assaulted by a ram, which did not readily give up. The players tried to beat their assailant off with golf clubs but found this a losing battle, so they took refuge behind a nearby tree. The ram persisted in its pursuit of the two, and finally, in frustration, they gave up, abandoning their game, and retiring somewhat sheepishly to the safety of the bar.

Returning just briefly to the question of the elephant caveat about right of way and inherent danger, we're unclear why the same principle did not apply in the case of the buffalo at the tee area. One certainly would have been disinclined to seek the beasts' permission to play through. Seemingly, they constituted a genuine danger to the two players.

That peculiar outside-agency status is usually invoked when the four-footed or winged beasts are guilty of carrying away golf balls. Dogs and crows are commonly wrongdoers, although children on bicycles and other casual passersby have also been known to play the role of outside agency.

I have personally witnessed crows at Carnoustie, on the east coast of Scotland north of St. Andrews, for some unknown reason swoop down and snatch up a golf ball and carry it for dropping in the adjacent British military armament range.

Indeed, a few years ago, seagulls became a problem in the northeastern section of the United States, apparently mistaking golf balls for some edible shellfish. A bird would swoop down, as they did in great numbers at a driving range in Connecticut, pick up a ball and carry it out above the rocks along the shore, where it would drop the ball, seeming to believe the ball would crack on the rocks and expose edible meat for the bird. Luckily, at a driving range such animal behavior did not involve any Decisions.

Confusion over the identity of golf balls by animals is not uncommon. Workers a few years ago found a neat stack of golf balls in the woods; apparently, some woodland animal thought they were eggs, ideal for the coming winter's menu. And a chicken was seen in Scotland actually sitting on a golf ball (the Eden Course, in St. Andrews), either hoping it would hatch or enthralled by the thought of having laid a dimpled egg.

Outside Heidelberg, Germany, conspicuously along the par-five fourteenth hole, it was commonplace for German elders to walk along a road paralleling the fairway on the left side, genially watching the crazy American military personnel playing their funny game, and cheerfully tossing back any golf balls that trickled out of bounds near them. Often, their dogs were with them and played the role of ball recoverer. Children on bicycles also would pick up the golf balls and pedal hurriedly away with the ball in hand or stuffed in a pocket. They doubtless would sell them later to other American players for a couple of deutsche marks.

All of them, elders, dogs, and kids, were outside agencies and likely to remain so.

In the case of the dogs and the crows, the player may drop a ball at a point as close as possible to where the animal (our infamous outside agency) picked up the original ball, and, without penalty, play away.

It is amazing how quickly animals may change their identities; for example, geese on golf courses are commonplace in the eastern United States, and if they are merely wandering around the golf course, and one of them happens to ruin your golf shot by getting hit in a rather undignified location, that is the rub of the green—simply tough luck—and no relief is forthcoming.

It happened to Ron Benko at the Fiddler's Elbow Golf Club in Bedminster, New Jersey. His ball deflected into a nearby pond even though the drive that had caught the rear end of this huge goose had been well clear, to the right, of the water hazard. Benko sought relief, but when the official edict came down, the verdict was rub of the green, which ended any possible debate. Benko was forced to accept his penalty, and the goose, presumably somewhat the worse for wear, waddled away.

Animals have been known to become victims, too, and not come away as healthy as that broad-beamed fowl. At the eighteenth hole of St. Margaret's-at-Cliffe Golf Club in Kent, England, W. J. Robinson, a professional, teed off as a cow foolishly ambled across the fairway perhaps a hundred yards in front of the tee area. The ball caught the poor beast in the back of the head. She collapsed on the spot, hauled herself uncertainly to her feet, and staggered perhaps fifty yards before falling again, dead.

Earlier, we alluded to the burrowing character of animals. Relief is granted in some instances if a ball comes to rest, or is believed to be lodged, in a hole dug by a burrowing animal. "Burrowing animal" is the key phrase. It isn't sufficient for the ball to find a hole made by a digging animal; it must be the hole of an animal designated as a "burrowing animal," such as a rabbit or mole, or even certain reptiles, creatures who burrow homes in which they live. Salamanders and crawfish are both regarded officially as burrowing animals. But if your ball comes to rest in a hole dug by a dog, that's just tough luck, Charlie.

Clearly, this presents a problem; how does one go about determining the nature of the digger possibly years after the deed has been done? That is a good question, better submitted to the experts. The USGA's Director of Rules and Competitions, Tom Meeks, said that in his opinion, if there was some doubt about the nature of the burrower, he would take the conservative position that relief should not be permitted.

Apart from Rules and Decisions, animals may show up on golf courses and affect the character of play in ways subtle and unsubtle without forcing any regulatory judgment.

Roadrunners, odd birds common to the desert-like regions of the United States and familiar to film-cartoon fans everywhere, have a peculiar mating ritual, which, for reasons known only to roadrunners, they often like to conduct at greenside.

A player at Borrego Springs, in southern California, wrote to the USGA about this exotic sexual practice by the birds. It goes something like this: The male roadrunner will catch a lizard. Reptile in beak, he then seeks out the female of his choice. He offers her this juicy morsel, but only if she will first submit to his romantic blandishments. This ritual is often consummated beside the green at the course in Borrego Springs, to the considerable distraction of bemused players. After consummation, the male will turn over the lizard to the female roadrunner, and she will carry it away for her dining pleasure.

31

It doesn't need to be said that this romantic interlude can be unnerving to someone lining up a putt, and have many a golfer wishing that Wile E. Coyote would make a quick appearance.

Even frogs have contributed their wrinkles to golf courses. During one match, a player stroked his chip shot into the hole; the ball popped out almost immediately, closely followed by a large, chagrined frog. In another case, a talented young player was playing his qualification round for a tournament in southern California when he hit a shot into the rough on the left. The ball kicked into an open pipe protruding from the ground, seemingly an impossible situation. But no, the pipe had been home for a frog. The distracted amphibian pushed upward, and the ball tumbled safely out ahead of it, thus saving the player some confusing Decision making.

Animals, furred and feathered, affect golf in other ways, especially during these days of tireless environmental concern. When the Northern California Golf Association was having its course, Poppy Hills Golf Club, built on the steep slopes within Pebble Beach, on California's Monterey Peninsula, birds and beasts were constant factors that kept Robert Trent Jones Jr., the architect, and John

Zoller, then the NCGA executive director, filling out countless forms for governmental agencies.

For example, a tall dead tree had to be maintained in the wooded rough to the left of the ninth green because it was home to the hairy owl. Moreover, certain other little woodland creatures were protected during the course-building stages by restrictions on removal of stumps and dead logs.

Evidence notwithstanding, animals of many varieties may be hazardous to players of the game of golf, and if questions pop up about God's beasts of the woods and of the fields, most of the inquiries should be answered under the Rule of equity.

II

OH, GOD! NATURE AND OTHER DISTRACTIONS

Some players would complain if they were playing on Dolly Parton's bedspread.

—**JIMMY DEMARET**, *Golf Magazine*, 1983

35

The outdoor character of golf means that sooner or later every player will find himself or herself cautiously studying the elements, from weather to nature's other equally unpredictable faces in their myriad expressions. Most golfers have a healthy apprehension when confronted by the onset of a thunderstorm. At times, it seems that God has taken an active dislike to the game and its players.

Ask Lee Trevino, who was one of three players to be struck by lightning together during a tournament a few years ago (the others were Jerry Heard and Bobby Nichols). He and his playing companions were hospitalized but, luckily, were none the worse for wear. With typical Trevino wit, he said he now has a perfect solution for any future storm—he carries a one-iron, because "even God can't hit a one-iron."

During that same occasion, England's Tony Jacklin had a club wrenched from his hand by a bolt and hurled some fifteen feet.

Two years later, in separate 1977 tournaments in Europe, lightning again paid visits and hit two well-known players, although neither was seriously injured. Britain's Mark James, in the Swiss Open, and Severiano Ballesteros, in the Scandinavian Open, were both struck by lightning.

But a storm indirectly contributed a new Decision for 1991 to the ever-growing book. In 1987, play was suspended during the Sammy Davis Greater Hartford Open when a thunderstorm passed through. Competitors were told that play would resume at a specified time, and a siren would sound to call them back on the course.

Unfortunately, Japanese golfer Aki Ohmachi's command of English was limited, so he did not understand what was happening. When he saw several players walking down an adjacent fairway, he thought play had been resumed, so he began to play again, two minutes too soon, and he was disqualified.

In the wake of this incident, it was agreed by several PGA officials as well as by USGA and Royal and Ancient decision-makers that the punishment was too severe. Now, in stroke play competition, the Committee is justified to modify the disqualification penalty to two strokes or, if circumstances warrant, to waive it entirely under Rule 33-7 ("A penalty of disqualification may in exceptional individual cases be waived, modified or imposed if the Committee considers such action warranted.").

In a sense, one might suppose, nature is being overridden by the rational side of the human mind. Yet there's an overlooked irony in the Decisions book as well as in the Rules of Golf; many of the offbeat facets of Rules and Decisions are embraced within an esoteric category called *equity*. That is well and good, but equity is not included among those legislative ingredients explained in the Definitions sections of the Rules and the Decisions books.

So what is equity, and what is its relationship with God's incursions into this goofy game of ours?

In the absence of a solid and terribly official Definition from the game's congressmen, we would identify equity as fairness of judgments governing playing issues not expressly covered by strongly defined Rules or Decisions. When in doubt, try equity. Many of the Rules and Decisions involving animals, God's creatures, reasonably fall under equity, such as the ever-unpopular rattlesnake in the bunker (see Chapter I, Animals: Of Feathers and Fur . . .), hazards (see Chapter V, Hazards to Your Health), and outside agencies (scattered generously through this volume). Even obstructions show up under equity, and here's a classic example that reflects very well the fairness element central to equity.

A player found his ball resting on the cart path, from which he wanted to take relief under Rule 24-2b(i). Unfortunately, the nearest point for relief was in a large puddle of casual water (any temporary accumulation of water not in a water hazard), which wasn't what he had in mind.

Nonetheless, he dropped his ball in the casual water as stipulated under the applicable Rule. He then looked legitimately for a point of relief, this time from the casual water. Unfortunately, his nearest point of relief under Rule 25-1b(i) would be back on the cart path. So what were his options, if he had any?

Fairness rears its pretty little head. "In addition to his available options under the Rules, in equity (Decision, Rule 1–4/8) he may obtain relief without penalty as follows: The point on the course nearest to where the ball originally lay on the cart path shall be determined which (a) is not nearer the hole, (b) avoids interference by both the cart path and the casual water, and (c) is not in a hazard or on a putting green. The player shall lift the ball and drop it within one club-length of the point thus determined on ground that fulfills (a), (b), and (c) above."

If the dropped ball rolls into a position where there is interference by either the cart path or the casual water, Rule 20-2c applies. That Rule spells out when a ball may be re-dropped without penalty, including the above described situation.

Harry Bradshaw, a fine player out of Kilcroney, in Dublin, Ireland, some years ago, found himself confronted by a difficult situation during the 1949 British Open Championship at Royal St. George's, Sandwich, England, when his golf ball came to rest inside a broken beer bottle at the fifth hole during the second round. A no-nonsense man with little patience for pondering things, he stepped right up and swung at the ball, sending shards of broken glass flying every which way. Mercifully, no one was hurt, including Bradshaw. But the question logically arose as to whether he was entitled to relief from what was clearly a dangerous situation.

It was later reported that he had been worried that if he treated it as an unplayable lie—his thought—it might result in a disqualification. His broken-bottle shot traveled about thirty yards; that bottle cost him dearly, as he took a 6 at the par-four hole. He finished that Open tied with Bobby Locke, but he lost a thirty-six-hole playoff to Locke by twelve strokes. Bradshaw lost the British Open by a broken beer bottle.

Whatever the applicable Rule in Bradshaw's day, Rule 24-1b now governs the situation under the category of movable obstruction. The Rule reads: "If the ball lies in or on the obstruction, the ball may be lifted, without penalty, and the obstruction removed. The ball shall *through the green* or in a *hazard* be dropped, or on the *putting green* be placed, as near as possible to the spot directly under the place where the ball lay in or on the obstruction, but not nearer the hole. The ball may be cleaned when lifted under Rule 24-1."

Bradshaw would have spared his golf club and avoided possible serious injury under 24-1b.

Another branch of the obstructions legislation is 24-2, which involves immovable obstructions. The peculiar case mentioned in the Introduction of the player who hit his ball into the clubhouse bar and opened the window to make his shot is controlled by Decision 24-2/14.

A variation on this theme came up on what had to be a rustic golf course that featured a barn adjacent to one of the fairways. The door on the tee side was open, and when the player's tee shot bounded into the barn, the next question logically was, could he open the barn door at the opposite end of the structure and continue his tortuous trip to the green that way? The answer is yes, he could. The barn, like the clubhouse in the related case, is an immovable obstruction, but the door, like the window, is not. One of its functions is to open. This became Decision 24-2/15.

Subsequent to the Bradshaw issue, yet another question arose, and it is one that must beleaguer players everywhere. Even if you religiously carry Rules and Decisions books in your golf bag, and your ball comes to rest in a beer bottle, à la Bradshaw, where do you look in your portable library to learn the proper procedure?

A point made often—and wisely—is that players may very well benefit by knowing the Rules and Decisions (usually more easily said than done between understanding the verbiage and finding the fitting legislation in the first place). Not only can you avoid penalty situations such as those that cost Craig Stadler dearly in 1987 in the infamous building-a-stance-on-a-towel incident in the San Diego Open, but also because you may have a legitimate recourse to the Rules—or Decisions—for penalty-free relief from awkward situations. God may not always smile on golfers, but it has been known to happen now and then.

Many of us have witnessed some version of this difficulty. You or one of your companion players hits a shot, and the ball strikes a power pole that is part of an electric line traversing the golf course. The ball bounds into a wholly undesirable location after it hits the pole.

You may find that a Local Rule applies, allowing you to retrieve your ball and try again without penalty. The power line is not a part of the golf course, so you are spared the inadvertent misfortune of being penalized because the pole was there for the striking.

A local committee, however, may wish to apply this Local Rule only to specific situations, e.g., power lines that traverse the line of play, but not those that run parallel.

After the USGA and Royal and Ancient were asked whether a Local Rule could allow a player whose ball is deflected by this power line to replay the stroke *if he wishes* without penalty, Decision 33-8/13 said no. However, a Local Rule *requiring* a player to replay the stroke would be acceptable.

But we've strayed from the impact certain twists of the Almighty have on the game of golf—and He somehow always manages to be there. Indeed, a veritable sub-category of golf jokes has sprung up as testimony to the relationship between God and golf.

A somewhat peculiar *use* of nature, God's most ubiquitous face within the game, is the casting of one's shadow over the ball as it hangs on the lip of the hole. Grass normally is drawn toward the sun, an immutable law of nature, so by cutting off the sun's rays, the player anticipates the grass blades will bend and allow the ball to fall into the hole. Is this tinkering with nature considered improper or incorrect? Is the player in breach of Rule 1-2, exerting an influence on the ball?

No. There is a caveat, however; there's a limit of a reasonable amount of time, or the player becomes guilty of delaying play. This happened to Denis Watson during the 1985 United States Open at Oakland Hills, in Birmingham, Michigan. You may give your scam a whirl, but do not dilly-dally.

45

A dramatic act of God made itself felt on October 17, 1989, in California, when a major earthquake rattled much of the central state at 5:04 P.M. It not only did considerable damage to clubhouses and golf courses, notably in the Santa Cruz Mountains, but also affected the play of the game at the height of the quake's activity.

A young, would-be professional was playing a qualifying round on the Bayonet course at Fort Ord Army base, just north of Monterey, when the quake struck. He was in the process of attempting a delicate little chip shot from the raised back edge of an elevated green. His lightly tapped shot landed on the green when the heaving began. When he had sufficiently recovered his composure after fifteen seconds or so of stark terror, the player saw that his golf ball now lay an estimated twenty-five yards beyond the green, down the sloped fairway.

What was his recourse? Another shot from the point where he had struck his original shot? Afraid not. He had just experienced one of the more awesome bum breaks in golf history. An earthquake is not an outside agency.

46

III

CADDIES: THOSE LEFT HOLDING THE BAGS

Player: "Can I reach it with a
five-iron?"
Caddie: "Eventually."

—JOHN ADAMS,
first playing Prestwick,
in Scotland

47

Caddies are a subject unto themselves. Lines by caddies have brightened the literature of golf immeasurably, and their frequent richness of character has embellished the professional golf tours to a point that even those in the galleries and in front of TV sets know Herman Mitchell (Lee Trevino's long-time caddie) on sight.

Their senses of humor may occasionally be overrated, but the lines often attributed to them are sufficiently priceless that a book devoted solely to caddie stories has been published. (By the way, the film *Caddyshack* notwithstanding, caddie is spelled with an "ie" ending, not a "y." A *caddy* is a container used to hold tea bags or pencils; a *caddie* carries golf clubs. Don't ask why; that is correct, and that should be enough.) No less an expert than Alistair Cooke corrected William Safire in public print over the spelling of *caddie* (in fairness to Safire, the correction was printed in his own *New York Times* column).

As for caddie humor, the response was exemplary when Harry Vardon, a superlative player who still holds the record with six British Open Championships, wasn't playing well and was unsure which club to use, so he asked his caddie, "What should I take here?" and the caddie promptly replied, "Well, sir, I'd recommend the 4:05 train."

In terms of Rules and Decisions, caddies should be thought of as extensions of their players. Indeed, caddies can get their players into trouble in a variety of ways. Eddie Martin caddied for Byron Nelson in the 1946 Open at Canterbury, and when Martin stumbled carrying Nelson's heavy golf bag as he ducked under the marshals' ropes at the thirteenth hole, he fell into Nelson's ball. Nelson was penalized one stroke and, as it turned out, wound up in a playoff with Lloyd Mangrum and Vic Ghezzi. They needed two playoff rounds to settle the outcome, and Mangrum won. That lone penalty stroke was disastrous for Nelson.

It is more likely to be some breach of the Rules or Decisions, however, that involves the caddie rather than the chance accident that must have bedeviled Martin's memory for years.

For example, Decision 20-2c/4 decrees that a player could lose a hole in match play or sustain a two-stroke penalty in stroke play if the caddie deliberately stopped a dropped ball prematurely.

How about this one? In a stroke-play tournament, A, with a caddie, was playing with fellow competitor B, pulling a trolley on a course familiar to A but unfamiliar to B. The caddie was too small to carry two bags. At a certain blind hole for an approach shot B asked A's caddie the distance, but before B got any answer from A's caddie, A intervened, saying that B infringed Rule 9-1 even though he got no answer and hence no benefit in determining the play in any way whatever.

Is B interpreted as having infringed Rule 9-1 ("The number of strokes a player has taken shall include any penalty strokes incurred.")? Is that the meaning implied therein? By asking A's caddie the distance, B violated Rule 9-1, was the reply, even if he did not get the answer. (Advice regulations now fall under Rule 8, not 9.)

An odd variation on the Decision about asking advice from a caddie occurred in this country. A player surveying his putt saw a caddie from the corner of his eye, and he thought it was his caddie. He asked which way the ball would fall on the putt. Looking up, he realized the caddie was not his and quickly instructed him not to answer his question.

Nonetheless, his kindly spirited opponent claimed the hole based on Rule 9-1a. Later, the committee disallowed the claim, and the USGA agreed with the committee's decision.

Caddies can earn their players penalties by standing so as to block the glare of the setting sun, and it is unacceptable to use a caddie as a shield from the wind, or to have a caddie hold a protective umbrella against wind or rain. Indeed, a caddie may not cast a shadow in a line that indicates the route for the player's putt. That is not permissible.

Caddies must be more than merely long suffering. Not only are they expected to endure the modest skills of some atrocious performers, but they must know the Rules of the game as well, to avoid the humiliation of costing their players penalty strokes for some wrongdoing. All of this, of course, they must accept while lugging around a golf bag that may be stuffed with a bottle or flask, a box of cigars, several dozen golf balls, a rain outfit, an extra pair of golf shoes, a course guide, sandwiches left over from the previous summer, and the full complement of fourteen golf clubs, plus a surplus of tees, pencils, ball markers, a slightly abused banana, and the like.

It goes with the territory of playing caddie.

It is wrong to think it is easy to be a caddie. Some years ago, a young man took on as his customer an irascible old fellow who was as good hearted as they come but had a monumental temper, most often directed at himself when his shots went awry.

During his round, he badly sliced a shot that headed for deep woods to the right of the fairway. It came immediately after one of his playing partners had sliced a shot that struck a tree and bounded back on the fairway, to the voluble consternation of the red-faced, white-haired man. When his shot followed suit but did not rebound to the fairway, the cursing was awesome.

The young caddie set off in the approximate direction of his patron's shot. He disappeared into the woods. Minutes crept past, and there was no sign of the young man. Finally, the player called—not unkindly—for the lad to come out. This set off a god-awful caterwauling.

53

The player went into the woods and located the youth. "Did you find the ball?" he asked. This triggered an even greater wailing from the young man.

"What in the world is wrong?" the old man asked. "All I asked is whether you found the ball. If you didn't, it is not a crisis. I'll drop another."

The tears continued to flow as the boy said, "I've lost your clubs!"

The peculiar role of caddies as, in effect, partners with their employers creates some novel predicaments. For example, a passerby—an outside agency—at a golf course picked up a stray drive and tossed it back on the course. Moreover, the observer notified the caddie of what he had done. The player then played the ball from its in-bounds position. He was penalized two strokes for playing a wrong ball. The caddie should have notified the player, if possible, before he hit.

What would the ruling be if neither the player nor the caddie knew the ball had been thrown back on the course? In equity, there would be no penalty for playing a wrong ball (Rule 15). If the player had discovered before playing from the new teeing ground that his original ball was out of bounds, he would have had to go back and play another ball under penalty of one stroke (Rule 27-1). If the discovery was not made until later than this, the score with the wrong ball would stand.

At one time, working as a caddie was a common form of employment for young Americans. It seems to have fallen into disfavor over the past few decades. Although more golf is being played today, the youngsters have been supplanted largely by the mechanized golf carts that clutter both public and private courses in America. In Great Britain and Ireland, where mechanized carts are almost unheard of, there is no shortage of caddies waiting in the wings for employment. Moreover, most of them are knowledgeable not only about the Rules but about the courses.

A few years ago, my playing companion had hired a caddie, Bob, for the first round at St. Andrews Old Course. On the twelfth hole, a par four, I had the honor and hit what I thought was a perfect shot. I had played the Old Course a few years before, but I had forgotten many of the details. As I watched my unerring shot, my friend's caddie said, "Too bad about that. Nicely struck, too." Huh?

He was right, of course; just over the crest in mid-fairway lay a large bunker. Bob warned his client, who faded a trifle to the right but was quite safe.

Caddies, perhaps, have played a less prominent role within the game during the past few years—hence, figuring less in the Decisions, or at least no more than they did twenty years ago. If they're going to show up anywhere today, it more likely would be on one of the proliferating professional tours—PGA, LPGA, Senior, Ben Hogan—or one of the burgeoning satellite events, to mention nothing about the overseas tours, which may appeal to adventuresome linguists among American bag-carriers. For one thing, naturally, there's more money to be made caddying on this tour or that. Ten percent, or more, from one of those fat checks for the players will buy a wealth of groceries and walking shoes for a caddie.

It was noticeable that among the dozen or so Decisions that became effective in 1990, not one involved a caddie in even the most indirect way. Indeed, save for the rarefied atmosphere of the tours, caddies may be regarded accurately as an increasingly endangered species in this country. Thus, the gradual disappearance of references to caddies from the Decisions book should be viewed as logical.

At least, this is generally true in America. Caddies still proliferate in the United Kingdom, where young and old alike can be seen hauling golf bags for a living, and where it is even a problem for the aged because the government takes a dim view of their golf earnings if they're also receiving a regular income from taxpayers through retirement.

The few remaining American caddies do not seem to enjoy the same panache.

IV

WHO GOES THERE? FRIEND OR ENEMY?

Never bet with anyone you meet on the first tee who has a deep suntan, a one-iron in his bag, and squinty eyes.

—DAVE MARR,
former PGA champion

When this chapter was envisioned, the thought was to focus on the rascal opposite you, the player with whom you had that wager, or against whom you were matched for the club championship or the local scramble tournament. For that matter, it might be no one more threatening than your wife or husband. Indeed, with early retirements and the trendy move to the nation's Sunbelt, golf within married couples has become far more prevalent these days than it once was.

Realistically, golf is a game that may be played comfortably regardless of age or gender, and it is a game ideally suited to those whose children have grown, leaving spare time for Mom and Dad and the pleasure of doing something together.

But the friend-or-enemy concept surfaces in yet another way, although it is almost exclusively a factor touching the golf lives of professional players, that is, those who attract galleries. You and I probably do not fall into that bracket; only a masochist would care to watch me in action.

Spectators limit themselves chiefly to the better players, professionals primarily, and amateurs competing either in national championships or well publicized regional competitions.

Lest you presume foolishly that spectators are lost in the shuffle of golf's Decisions, think again. It isn't so.

A classic instance occurred in the early years of The Masters Tournament in Augusta, Georgia, when Gene Sarazen stroked an approach shot to the eighteenth green, and it came to rest beneath the skirt of a young woman seated on the back edge of the green.

Before the somewhat delicate matter was officially resolved, the young woman was forced to stand and jiggle just a bit before the crowded gallery until Sarazen's golf ball fell free. Isaac B. "Ike" Grainger, a member of the Augusta National Golf Club and a Rules official at the scene, reported: "By this time, players, officials, and gallery were in stitches, laughing. Tears were running down my face. I could hardly see." Sarazen subsequently dropped his ball, chipped close, and made his putt for par.

In this instance, the young woman would doubtless be identified as a friend of Sarazen's, rather than as an enemy. One has no idea where his shot might have finished were it not for her intercession.

Effective in 1990, a Decision was made governing a situation in which a ball was deliberately deflected or stopped through the green by a spectator.

Q: A player overshoots a green. A spectator (X) who is standing behind the green deliberately deflects or stops the ball. According to the Note under Rule 19-1, equity applies. What is the equitable procedure in this case?

A: In a case where the ball might have come to rest where X was situated if he had not deliberately deflected or stopped it, the player should be required to drop a ball at the spot where X was situated. For example, if another spectator (Y) had been behind X, the ball might have struck Y if X had avoided it, and come to rest where X was located.

If there is no question that the ball would have come to rest somewhere else if X had not deflected or stopped it, the committee must make a judgment as to where the ball would have come to rest, giving the player the benefit of any doubt. For example, if no person or object had been behind X and without any doubt the ball would have come to rest either in a lateral water hazard behind the green or in the rough just short of the hazard, the committee should require the player to drop the ball in the rough just short of the hazard.

The word *deliberate* may cause some future problems, however; the situation at The Masters could hardly be described as a deliberate effort on the part of the young woman to tamper with Sarazen's shot.

Children occasionally get into the act. Christy O'Connor Jr., was victimized when his ball was taken by a young boy, unknown to O'Connor, who presumed it was a lost ball. He accepted the penalty, of course, and finished in a tie for first place in the Penfold Tournament at Queen's Park, Bournemouth, eventually losing in a playoff.

Crowd interference has even affected golf history. In 1930, Bob Jones and Cyril Tolley were playing the seventeenth hole at St. Andrews Old Course in the British Amateur. Jones's approach bounded into a mass of spectators, possibly keeping the ball from proceeding to the roadway behind the hole. It saved the hole for Jones, who went on to defeat Tolley and, months later, to complete the Grand Slam by winning the British Amateur and Open and the U.S. Amateur and Open.

Finally, during the 1983 Suntory World Match Play Championship, Nick Faldo hit his approach into a massed crowd around the green. To the consternation of Australia's Graham Marsh, Faldo's shot was tossed onto the green by an anonymous member of the packed gallery. The official insisted that Faldo play the thirty-foot putt. He needed just two putts, while his unnerved opponent, Marsh, three-putted and subsequently lost the match, 2 and 1.

A ball coming to rest beneath someone's apparel is substantially different from the experience endured in 1986 by Dave Houpt, an American army sergeant playing in a tournament conducted annually by the *Stars and Stripes* military newspaper at the golf course of the Grand Ducal de Luxembourg. The tournament was in its thirtieth year in 1991.

The thirteenth hole at Luxembourg is awkward. Perhaps 160 yards off the tee, the main entrance and exit road from the highway to the clubhouse crosses, and drivers of arriving and departing automobiles have the careless habit of materializing without slowing down or exercising even routine caution.

So it was that Houpt teed off just as a car pulled out from the trees guarding the right side of the fairway from the clubhouse area, and Houpt's sharp drive caught the left rear window. He shattered it. The driver, an attractive Luxembourgian woman, was understandably startled, but she drove onward, out the gate and down the road.

Meanwhile, Houpt and his playing companions recovered from the shock of what had happened and debated the occurrence, concluding he should regard the car as an outside agency and drop a ball at a point on the teeing side of the roadway as close as possible to the point where his ball had hit the car.

Ironically, after Houpt had passed the road, the woman returned, broken window and all, and nerves still unsettled, went into the clubhouse to call her husband with a report about what had happened. After a much needed, relaxing drink, she struck up conversation with another woman, who was a stranger to her—by dumb chance, Houpt's patiently waiting wife, Kristina. Kristina Houpt was properly sympathetic, little realizing it was her own husband's golf ball that had struck this woman's automobile.

Upon returning from his round, Houpt said he was certain he had the longest drive in the tournament, although he did not recover his golf ball.

They still talk at the Klontarf course in Dublin, Ireland, about a shot on one of the back holes which borders a train track. The ball came to rest in a coal car en route to Belfast. Presumably the ball reached that city in Northern Ireland.

Another nominee for any long-drive contest is a shot hit in Bedfordshire, England; it landed in a vegetable truck and finally surfaced when the cabbages were unloaded at Covent Garden, forty miles away in London.

In 1955, at the Eden course in St. Andrews, Scotland, a player sliced a shot that disappeared into the open window of a passenger compartment in a passing train. Moments later, the ball reappeared, tossed back onto the fairway by a passenger, who waved a greeting as the train headed northward.

How about wagering? Betting sometimes seems endemic to the game, conspicuously in America, where some players insist they will not play golf if a bet isn't riding on the outcome.

Oddly enough, bets have produced some of the more amusing incidents within golf, although purists are often horrified by the swift appearance of wallets at first tees.

The nature of wagers, of course, goes far beyond the standard you-versus-me kind of thing. For example, in 1950, Bryan Field, vice president of the Delaware Park race course, insisted that, despite not having played golf in several years, he could tour difficult Pine Valley in less than three hundred shots. His scores at the first five holes were 7, 9, 4, 11, and 10, and it appeared his bet was won. It was; he finished with 148, less than half the wagered strokes. Moreover, he played the round in a comparatively quick two hours, fifty minutes.

John Ball, a gifted British amateur who was a key figure in the introduction to the game of the Haskell golf ball, toured Hoylake golf course, outside Liverpool, in a dense fog, in eighty-one shots and less than two and a quarter hours to win a wager. He used a black golf ball to counter the heavy fog.

When a hole at Forest Hills, New Jersey, was halved by two players who made holes-in-one, it produced a bet of $10,000 vs. $1 that it would not happen again during the wagering player's lifetime.

One of the more amusing bets involved the standard frightening cry of "Boo!" In England, again at Hoylake, which seems to attract novelty, a scratch player and an opponent with a six-handicap agreed to a match in which the six-handicap would play his rival even, but had the privilege of crying "Boo!" three times against the scratch player.

Anticipation won out. The six-handicap player used only one Boo!—at the thirteenth hole—but managed to win the match over the better player, who was fearfully awaiting the next outburst at every shot. The six-handicapper finished richer and with two Boos! still in hand.

Superficially, golf is a quiet, tranquil game that sometimes may take on a lonely character, yet over the years its players have been vulnerable to outside influence by others, ranging from opponents to galleryites, from casual passersby to caddies. The golf course may not be Grand Central Station, but it is hardly splendid isolation either.

Indeed, players outside your own group may become factors in your game, even to the point of evoking a ruling. This has happened. A group is playing very slowly. An impatient player in the following foursome becomes sufficiently angered that he hits into the slow group, narrowly missing one of the players. Now you have another angry golfer. Redfaced and reacting, he goes to the ball that almost struck him, takes out one of his clubs, and hits the ball back at the trailing group. The ball falls harmlessly beyond the following players.

Yet shouldn't a penalty be levied? After all, the slow player in the forward group hit the wrong ball, and quite knowingly. Well, yes. A penalty is in order, two strokes in stroke play and loss of the hole if the player whacking the ball back to its original striker is involved in a match. Moreover, what about the ideals of fair play in the episode? Shouldn't the act of angrily hitting into players ahead carry some penalty beyond the pain and suffering that may be inflicted when the two groups reach the clubhouse? That could degenerate into quite a profound donnybrook. Well, no; he could recover the returned shot and drop it as close as possible to the point from which he had originally struck the ball.

So much for any theorizing that golf is a game played in a vacuum, a bucolic setting where twittering birds and what P. G. Wodehouse called "the roar of butterflies" are the only sounds heard, and where a random deer emerging from the adjacent forest is a major invasion.

V

HAZARDS
TO YOUR
HEALTH

What's over there? A nudist colony?

—LEE TREVINO,
*after three partners drove
into the woods*

*I've lost balls in every hazard
and on every course I've tried,
but when I lose a ball in the ball
washer it's time to take stock.*

—MILTON GROSS,
*Eighteen Holes
in My Head, 1959*

71

Any clubhouse chatter about a player's worst round will invariably involve hazards. My own worst hole was a 23 taken at the par-three fifteenth hole at the Heidelberg military golf course in West Germany, where I hit a decent, slightly off-line tee shot that caught the upper edge of the bunker on the front left of the green, perhaps twenty feet from the flagstick. I finished the hole two bunkers and twenty-two strokes later with a thirty-foot putt. It was no honor to one-putt from thirty feet for that 23. It was a forgettable distinction.

Many things qualify as hazards, although most of us yammer in terms of sand and water. By extension, trees are hazards, and one might suppose that many alien items showing up on golf courses are hazards, or at least, hazardous.

Yet the Definitions offer a brief and explicit line: "A 'hazard' is any *bunker* or *water hazard*." The latter does split into two categories, however: plain, everyday water hazards; and lateral water hazards.

According to the Rules of Golf:

"A water hazard is any sea, lake, pond, river, ditch, surface drainage ditch, or other open water course (whether or not containing water) and anything of a similar nature. All ground or water within the margin of a water hazard is part of the water hazard. The margin of a water hazard extends vertically upwards and downwards . . . Stakes and lines defining the margins of water hazards are in the hazards. Water hazards, other than lateral water hazards, should be defined by yellow stakes or lines.

"A lateral water hazard is a water hazard or that part of a water hazard so situated that it is not possible or is deemed by the Committee to be impracticable to drop a ball behind the water hazard in accordance with Rule 26-1b. That part of a water hazard to be played as a lateral water hazard should be distinctively marked. Lateral water hazards should be defined by red stakes or lines."

Once these basic elements have been absorbed, and hopefully understood, the tough part begins. In 1982 at the Knollwood Club, north of Chicago, Jeff Ellis of Oak Harbor, Washington, was 1-down in the final match of the United States Mid-Amateur Championship when his ball trickled downward within the line marking the water hazard adjacent to the ninth fairway. Bill Hoffer, his adversary and the eventual champion, was having his own troubles. Ellis had room to stand between the water and the ball with a reasonable swing. Preoccupied, he reached down and picked up a harmless leaf, tossing it aside. It was a meaningless, nervous gesture.

Not so. It was grounds for a penalty. Instead of overtaking Hoffer and going to the final nine holes even, Ellis was suddenly 2-down and upset with himself for picking up a loose impediment within the boundary of the hazard. It may well have cost him the championship. Later, Herb Graffis, a feisty, witty old journalist who died at the age of ninety-two a few years ago, advised Ellis belatedly, "Young man, in the future, never pick up anything on the golf course unless it is green and negotiable."

Some years ago, a player hit his shot into a small, swiftly moving stream traversing a fairway not far from the green. He walked to where he had seen his ball roll out of sight and, presumably, into the water hazard. The water was clear, and only several inches deep, but no golf ball was visible. The ball had been carried by the water's flow downstream and out of bounds. That's a "Tough luck, Charlie" situation. Water is not an outside agency, so what you find is what you get, and the ball is out of bounds. It is little consolation that the Decisions recommend the installation of a screen to prevent this from happening.

Hazard-related incidents can take on a whimsical character, too. Subsequent to February 1971, when then-Captain Alan Shepard (since elevated to the rank of Admiral) used a multipurpose device equipped with a six-iron head to hit a golf shot on the moon, the Royal and Ancient Golf Club of St. Andrews, Scotland, sent Shepard a congratulatory note that read, in part: "Warmest congratulations to all of you on your great achievement and safe return. Please refer to Rules of Golf section on etiquette, paragraph 6, quote—'Before leaving a bunker a player should carefully fill up all the holes made by him therein', unquote."

The club used by Shepard on the moon is now on display at Golf House, the museum adjacent to headquarters for the USGA.

Another memorable bunker incident occurred at the Hamilton Golf Club, southeast of Glasgow, Scotland, and Lindsay Baxter, the Scot responsible, won't quickly forget it. His approach shot to the eighteenth hole, immediately behind the clubhouse, came to rest lying lightly atop the sand in a greenside bunker.

He marched into the bunker, took his stance, and swung. He caught all of the ball, lifting it in a high arc that almost cleared the clubhouse, landing on the far side of the roof and bouncing toward the crowded parking lot. Jim Orr, a club member, was loading his clubs into his car when he heard a loud report nearby. He wheeled in time to see a golf ball bound away after it had bounced off the roof of a parked car, leaving a telltale dent.

Almost immediately, Baxter appeared breathlessly around the corner. Spotting Orr, he asked, "Jimmy, did you see a ball fly over here?" Orr pointed, remarking, "Sure did. I heard it. You've left a tidy dent in that automobile's roof." Baxter followed Orr's pointing finger, then gave a sigh of relief. "Thank God. It's my car."

And as a final deviation from the formal hazards of water and sand: A hazard-fraught match was arranged in the south of England when a wager was made between a scratch player and a fellow with a high handicap. No strokes were given; they played level. There was a rub, however. The scratch player faced a novel requirement; he had to drink a whisky and soda at each tee.

The scratch player was 1-up when he collapsed at the tee of the sixteenth hole. According to later reports, he was not well for quite some time after his foolish wager. So, for practical purposes, he lost, 2-down, sacrificing the sixteenth to place the match all square, then forfeiting additionally the seventeenth and eighteenth holes.

The legitimate golf hazards, however, remain those of sand and water.

At the Geelong Golf Club in Australia, Tom Charteris hit a poor tee shot to the short second hole, which featured a creek with steep clay banks. His shot rolled over the nearest edge and down the bank toward the creek. He found his ball embedded in the gooey clay short of the water, so he elected to play it. Using a seven-iron, he tried to dig it out, but after he swung, the ball was nowhere in view.

When he prepared to clean his club and remove a mass of the viscous clay, he discovered his ball was in the middle of the goo. He was unable to shake it free. At last, he manually removed the ball, cleaned it, and dropped it behind the hazard—

without penalty. This procedure later was approved by the Royal and Ancient.

The water hazard occupied a prominent role in the 1984 U.S. Mid-Amateur Championship. The more marginal of decisions rendered by an official came in a third-round match between Bob Lewis, an eventual finalist, and Howard Logan. Lewis was two up entering the par-three fifteenth. He promptly teed off from the elevated tee area, and his ball drifted short and right, splashing into a small lake to the right and in front of the green. Logan, with ample time and a distinct advantage, drummed his tee shot safely to the back edge of the downward sloping green. His ball lay in fairly heavy grass, but it was manageable.

Because of the irregularly shaped left side of the water hazard where Lewis's ball had sunk to its grave, the question arose from where he should hit his third shot (including the penalty stroke). Lewis is aggressive, feisty, and as the beleaguered USGA official wandered somewhat aimlessly along the hazard's left margin, Lewis was right there in his wake, yapping at him. In essence, Lewis contended that his ball had come in high and drifted across the board wall of the water hazard, so he should be allowed his drop at a point where he would have a straight little pitch to the green. (Sitting behind the green during the entire episode, I saw the ball land in the water very close to the wall, impossible for a drifting shot described by Lewis. I was a reporter, however, not a Rules official, so my designated role was to shut up and stay out of it.)

Lewis's nattering seized the day. To Logan's disbelief, Lewis was permitted to drop a ball in a favorable position, and when he pitched up and one-putted for a four, Logan was reduced to chipping down just past the hole, from where he two-putted; they halved the hole. Later, after a 3 and 2 loss, Logan confessed that his distress was a result of the intimidation of an official by Lewis. In his view, that should never happen. He's right, of course.

This was a judgment call on the part of an official. Judgments rendered by players can also be beneficial—or disastrous.

In a semifinal match during that same Championship, David Jacobsen, brother of Peter Jacobsen, a PGA Tour professional, probably shot himself out of the final with a judgment call, again involving a water hazard. Holding a one-up lead over Mike Podolak, the eventual Mid-Amateur Champion, as they entered the monstrous eighteenth hole at the Atlanta

Athletic Club, Jacobsen was all but handed a spot in the final match when Podolak hit his second shot into a water hazard directly in front of the green. This 462-yard, par-four hole is famous for the great five-iron shot hit by Jerry Pate to win the 1976 U.S. Open.

So, unless he holed out his fourth shot, Podolak was looking at a five, at best, and all Jacobsen needed was to halve the hole and the match was his, as well as the berth in the final match against Bob Lewis the next day.

What did Jacobsen do? He went for the green—and failed to reach it. He, too, went into the drink. Now the officials had their forgettable moments in the limelight as they sought to determine who was farther away, thus, who should shoot first.

It was decided that Jacobsen's ball in the hazard was farther from the hole, so he dropped behind the hazard and prepared to hit first, although Podolak dropped much farther back, away from the hole. Because his ball entered the right side of the hazard, Jacobsen was prevented from moving back by trees flanking the right side of the fairway. Subsequently, his babied pitch shot also fell into the hazard. Stunned, Podolak then stroked his full wedge to the left fringe, where he lay four while Jacobsen was now hitting six. Podolak won the hole with six to Jacobsen's eventual eight.

So Jacobsen lost the match on the nineteenth hole with a bogey when he caught a greenside bunker with his approach shot.

Hazards have that name for a good reason. They aren't intended to make life any easier, and the premium, of course, lies in avoiding them at all costs.

VI

HOME SWEET OBSTRUCTIONS

The golfer has more enemies than any other athlete. He has 14 clubs in his bag, all of them different; 18 holes to play, all of them different, every week; and all around him are sand, trees, grass, water, wind, and 143 other players. In addition, the game is 50 percent mental, so his biggest enemy is himself.

—DAN JENKINS,
Sports Illustrated, 1982

Mildred "Babe" Didrikson Zaharias was not only a superb player in her abbreviated prime, she was also a smart player, constantly thinking her way around the playing field of her choice, whether it was a track or a golf course.

In the early 1950s, during an LPGA tournament being played in the northeastern part of this country, Zaharias found herself in an odd predicament. Her second shot came to rest to the left of the green on a par-five hole, meaning she should be in a fine position for a possible birdie.

Between her ball and the green, however, was a small but heavy piece of statuary. It was directly in line with the flagstick. Her question for reigning officialdom was this: Shouldn't she be allowed relief from this piece of stone froufrou?

After some learned debate among the LPGA experts on hand, it was decided that this immovable obstruction was, in truth, part of the golf course, so the Babe should not be allowed any relief.

Immovable? Zaharias thought this one over, then turned to the gallery, where her powerful wrestler husband was quietly trailing her playing group.

"George?" said the Babe, "Do you think you could move this little statue?"

He allowed that he could, and did. She chipped onto the green close by the hole, and sunk the putt for her birdie.

So much for that obstruction.

Obstructions take many forms. Under Definitions, here's what is said about them:

> An "obstruction" is anything artificial, including the artificial surfaces and sides of roads and paths, except:
>
> a. Objects defining *out of bounds*, such as walls, fences, stakes and railings;
>
> b. Any part of an immovable artificial object which is out of bounds; and
>
> c. Any construction declared by the Committee to be an integral part of the course.

Although golf cart manufacturers probably would not care to see their products represented as obstructions of any sort, they must be classified as movable ones by their very nature.

Clearly, the statuary figured in the Definition, but the question hinged on its movability. Zaharias proved it was not an immovable artificial object. Unfortunately for most women players, they aren't always accompanied by someone with George Zaharias's strength. That immediately broadens the range of movability.

We have discussed in the introduction the marvelous case of movability in an English clubhouse, when the player shuffled the bar furniture around quite correctly, but then erred (at the time) by opening a window in the bar, thus "improving his line of play." It was pointed out that this Decision has now been modified so that the player isn't faced with the requirement that he break the window to realize his shot.

Obstructions and obstacles seem to take an endless variety of form and character, some almost entertaining if you aren't the player facing the problem or a major golf Decision.

It was tough to fight off a smile in July, 1985, at the U.S. Women's Open, at the Baltusrol Golf Club in Springfield, New Jersey, when Sally Little hit her approach to the par-four fourteenth hole only to have the ball take one hop directly into a well-filled trash basket. Almost as though to add insult to injury, her ball was clearly visible, and identifiable as hers, through the wire netting of the basket.

Fishing among the soft-drink and beer bottles, hot-dog wrappers, and other debris routinely found in and around spectator sports events, she recovered her ball. The basket was moved, she took a drop, and other than perhaps a trace of embarrassment, she suffered no further damage.

Oddly enough, at the same hole, Beth Daniel earlier had sought relief from the roots of a large tree near the green (saying that adjacent bleachers were a temporary immovable obstruction), but her appeal was rejected.

Playing at the Hanau golf course in Germany, Bob Wicker hit a low line drive off the first tee—it was unlike him to stroke a low shot—and it cracked into one of the forward tee markers, bounding high over his head and into dense woods directly behind him. Ignoring his playing companion's genial observation that he was away, Wicker was forced to march into the wilderness, find his ball, and thrash his way out on perhaps the Hanau course's easiest golf hole, a 280-yard par-four.

As observed earlier, obstructions take a variety of forms.

While the professionals may play most PGA Tour courses at their maximum length, they also benefit from some things that the rest of us aren't likely to experience—the presence of grandstands and the ubiquitous television cables strung like so much spaghetti beside fairways and throughout the rough. These cables, by the way, are movable obstructions.

In the 1980 United States Open, played on the Lower Course at Baltusrol, Tom Weiskopf was en route in the first round to a record-tying 63 (sharers: Johnny Miller, 1973 Open at Oakmont; and Jack Nicklaus, the same day at Baltusrol). Weiskopf pushed his second shot at the lengthy par-five seventeenth hole just off the fairway. He found his ball in a tangle of ABC-TV cables, and relief from the problem was forthcoming. Few golfers enjoy run-ins with TV cables.

Perhaps a more conspicuous example of relief from an obstruction occurred during a more recent

Open, in 1984 at Winged Foot, in Mamaroneck, New York, where Greg Norman's tendency to hit his shots to the right was especially pronounced. Playing immediately ahead of Fuzzy Zoeller, and tied with him as they moved up the final hole, Norman again drifted his approach to the right, adjacent to the bleachers a few yards from the green. His was an impossible situation; he had no shot.

He was permitted relief from the oppressive grandstands, he was able to loft a little pitch out of the heavy grass, and the ball rolled across the green to the far edge. In fact, Zoeller had missed all the action and debate surrounding Norman's lie by the stands, so when Fuzzy came up and saw Norman lining up to putt, Zoeller thought his chief adversary lay two. Norman made the forty-foot putt. It was for his par, however, and when Zoeller two-putted to match that par, the two men were scheduled to return for a playoff, won by Zoeller.

Occasionally, an obstruction may thoroughly dominate a play. At the par-three sixteenth hole on the Coombe Wood Golf Club in England, a player hit a tee shot that flew into the vertical exhaust of a tractor which was being used to mow a nearby fairway. The tractor's operator noticed an inexplicable loss of power in his machine without knowing what had happened to account for it. Meanwhile, compression was building up in the exhaust system until the golf ball was suddenly forced out of the pipe at remarkable velocity, shooting high into the air.

The ball landed on the roof of a nearby home, from where it took a high bounce back onto the golf course, finally rolling to rest about three feet from the hole, an easy putt for a birdie once the stunned player had regained something approximating his composure.

Indeed, golf balls may wind up almost anywhere after flights that are often irregular, at best. Record books are jammed with oddities—golf balls finishing in the most unexpected locations. In London, a player found his golf ball inside an abandoned boot. It has not been uncommon for shots to go down chimneys and settle in fireplaces.

Obstructions may have a nebulous character. Tom Watson, discussing play from a bunker, pointed out, for example, that a twig—loose impediment because it is a natural object—may not be moved in a bunker if it happens to be interfering with a shot, but a cigar—an unnatural object and technically a movable obstruction—may be removed, even in a bunker.

The movable obstruction dictum within a hazard means you may clear away anything not natural—bottles, cigarette butts, cigars, a rake (of course), or a paper cup. As a rule, leave the natural stuff alone—even something as miniscule as a leaf, which did in Jeff Ellis during the 1982 U.S. Mid-Amateur final match.

If your ball should move during the process of removing a movable obstruction within a bunker, or any hazard, there is no penalty; simply replace the ball without penalty.

This, by the way, is the saving Decision applying when the professional tour players run up against TV cables, crowd-restraining ropes, and all the accoutrements related to professional tournaments.

It would seem to place a complicated premium on the player to determine what qualifies as natural or unnatural. It strikes me that a cigar arguably is natural because it is made of tobacco, one of nature's weeds. Yet a cigar is made by human beings, and that seems to be the persuasive argument.

There is a tendency toward confusion in dealing with immovable obstructions—what are a player's options? What may he reasonably do to get off the hook?

Suppose you are playing at Balcomie, southeast of St. Andrews, and your ball comes to rest just behind the jutting corner of the wooden building to the right of the first fairway, perhaps 175 yards off the tee—your ball rests perhaps an inch from the building's wall. Your shot toward the green is definitely impeded.

The point is this: if your ball lies on the obstruction, or if the obstruction interferes either with the area of your intended swing or with your stance, you are entitled to relief. The area of your intended swing should not be confused with your wanted line of flight toward the green. That is, if you have a clear swing and an unimpeded stance but the building is on the line toward the green, tough luck. After all, you hit the ball there.

A variation on this theme is a comparatively new limitation (1984) denying relief from immovable obstructions when one's ball is in a water hazard or lateral water hazard. Previously, bridges and artificially surfaced banks created more than their share of confusion. Now it is easy: either play the ball as it lies, or drop it out of the hazard with a one-stroke penalty.

For such details, however, we direct your attention to the authoritative book, *The New Rules of Golf*, illustrated and explained by Tom Watson, with Frank Hannigan, former USGA Senior Executive Director, who has doubtless had a hand in more than one Decision based on the Rules of Golf during his long career within the game. Watson and Hannigan focus on the no-nonsense side of the matter; the nonsense aspect is where all the fun lies.

Would this game of ours be nearly as much fun if someone didn't hit a tee shot into a barn adjacent to the golf course, then open the far door to continue the tortured trip to some distant, waiting green? Obstructions, too, doll up the golf scene and inspire table conversations.

Moreover, after all the words are stripped away, it is arguable that movable and immovable obstructions are a pair of categories that embody the worst enemy among obstructions—ourselves.

VII

PLEASE KEEP ON THE GRASS

I've been around golf courses all my life. They are the Demaret answer to the world's problems. When I get out on that green carpet called a fairway and manage to poke the ball right down the middle, my surroundings look like a touch of heaven on earth.

—JIMMY DEMARET,
My Partner, Ben Hogan, 1954

For some, golf is a stroll in the park. For others, such as Mark Twain. golf is a good walk spoiled. Bob Jones, who was among the finest players this country has produced, and a gifted writer on top of it, put the game into perspective when he wrote, "Golf is the most human of games. In it a man can become the hero of an unbelievable melodrama, the clown in a side-splitting comedy, the dogged victim of inexorable fate, all without having to bury a corpse or repair a tangled personality.'

Much hinges, of course, on an ability to keep on the grass—or, at least, to keep one's golf ball on the grass. Indeed, a warning about golf is inherent within the Rules of Golf. It is no accident that the word *fairway* appears nowhere within the Rules, nor in the Decisions, for that matter. (If it is any consolation, neither does the word *rough*.)

It is easy to infer that there is no such thing as a fairway in the game, and in truth, there are those golfers whose play leads observers inescapably to

conclusion. One of the most remarkable victo-
in a major competition achieved its notoriety
y because the winner found it utterly impossi-
keep his shots out of the rough. The player
was Severiano Ballesteros when he won the 1979
British Open at Royal Lytham/St. Annes.

Automobiles parked in fields adjacent to the
course were under constant threat by the Spaniard.
The only thing more remarkable than Ballesteros's
penchant to stray was his astonishing talent for recovery from the most improbable locations.

Normally, however, it is advisable to keep one's
golf ball on the short-cropped grass, or as it is more
properly known, "closely mown areas" (a nicety that
achieved coinage during the official debate over the
embedded ball Rule). In theory, at least, few evil
things are likely to happen when the ball is in clear
view.

Tendencies to abandon the safety of fairways
have served to introduce wayward players to rare
and even memorable experiences in that part of the
world commonly known as *rough*, in unofficial golf
parlance. Indeed, it is arguable that the world—and
life itself—has more rough than fairway to it, giving
an edge immediately to disaster.

Bunkers and bodies of water are discussed elsewhere in this study of masochism, and sand and water may be found readily without hitting off line. To reach the rough, however, usually demands a poor shot, and once its execution is realized, the player will find himself in forgettable surroundings. In this country, trees are a common curse; in Great Britain and Ireland, trees are supplanted on the great seaside courses—*links*—by *gorse*, that low, prickly blight known to the Scots as *whin*. A ball lodged in gorse may be visible, but fishing for it is almost a guarantee that you will be punctured by the thousands of long needles that characterize the foliage. Don't let the beautiful yellow flowers fool you; gorse is evil.

At some courses—and Lossiemouth on the coast of the Moray Firth, east of Inverness, comes immediately to mind—gorse *is* the rough. When you leave the fairway, you are automatically in gorse, just as at Portmarnock, north of Dublin, if you stray one foot off the fairway, you are in seagrass that will grab your club's head and turn it in your hand when you swing. Such doings give an astronomical look to one's scorecard.

Let's concentrate on America, however, where trees are high on the list of chief menaces to the innocent and unsuspecting player. Even visiting Scots notice this.

Robert Trent Jones Jr., the Palo Alto, California, golf architect, once referred to trees as "vertical hazards." It was an apt description, and if the Rules and Decisions books are any indication, trees are a profound ingredient in the modern game. Certainly, they are factored into course design, and anyone who has played the game has a tree memorable to his experience—usually in a negative way. It has been said, and written, far too often that trees should offer no problem because they're ninety percent air anyway.

Can anyone who has seen it forget the large tree that stands in mid-fairway of the seventeenth hole at the Cypress Point Club in Pebble Beach, California? One must believe that Alistair Mackenzie knew precisely what he was doing when he laid out that golf hole.

Indeed, trees have figured prominently in the layouts for United States Open Championships. In 1979, at the Inverness Club in Toledo, Ohio, a tree was deliberately planted during the Open to eliminate a short cut that Lon Hinckle had created to turn a dogleg par-five into a long par-four readily reachable in two shots from an adjoining fairway.

This full-grown, overnight tree effectively squelched Hinckle and his emulators, although the USGA was criticized for this belated, arbitrary stumbling block tossed in the path of an imaginative player.

Although disagreement about a tree at the fifth hole at the Medinah Country Club in Medinah, Illinois, is invariably triggered at the slightest mention of the subject, Medinah officials insist that the tree was planted as a result of the USGA's urgings before an Open a number of years ago, then criticized by the same USGA before the 1990 Open—as in, "What's that tree doing there?"

During the third round of the 1987 Open at the Olympic Club in San Francisco, Tommy Nakajima wound up in terrible trouble on the eighteenth hole when his second shot flew right and disappeared in the upper branches of a cypress tree. A teenage boy clambered into the tree but was unable to find and identify the ball. Nakajima, penalized stroke and distance for a lost ball, finished in a tie for ninth place, seven strokes behind Scott Simpson, the winner.

Trees assume perhaps a greater golf significance in the United States than they do in the United Kingdom because, generally speaking, we have so many more of them. Great Britain and Ireland have their parkland courses, but they seem to favor seaside golf far more than Americans.

This predilection for wooded golf is strongly reflected in our Rules and Decisions. Indeed, it creates a peculiar dimension to rulings. If a player believes his or her ball is lodged in a tree and shakes the tree, dislodging the ball, the penalty is one stroke for moving the ball. If the player fails to remove it from its resting place (which may not be all that easy to do if the tree is sufficiently flimsy that the ball could be shaken free), it costs two strokes or, in match play, loss of the hole. A more appealing alternative is to add a penalty stroke—a total of two—and declare the ball to be unplayable.

There is a correct way to dislodge and identify the golf ball, however; if a player states an intention to free his ball, identify it, and proceed under the ball-unplayable procedure, that is acceptable. It is also permissible to throw a club at the ball if desired (and the player isn't worried that it, too, may end up in an arboreal grave).

Arnold Palmer was playing in the Wills Masters Tournament in Melbourne, Australia, in 1984, when his hooked approach to the ninth green lodged in the crook of a gum-tree branch. Palmer climbed the tree and using the back of the club's head, he propelled the ball some thirty yards toward the green, chipped on, and one-putted for his par.

Trees have been a menace just by being there. In a recent national women's amateur event, a young woman lost a hole—and subsequently the match—when she broke a branch that was impeding her backswing.

Officials did not see it at the time, but learned of it later. What happened was this: Michelle Estill was a semifinalist in the United States Women's Amateur Public Links Championship, matched against Pearl Sinn, a teammate at Arizona State University though the two had never met in match play. At one point, Sinn was five under par and Estill four under. They were all square opening the eighteenth hole.

Estill's shot came to rest under a tree to the left of the fairway. A practice swing clipped a branch, which fell to the ground. Play continued as the match's referee and observer consulted with the Committee. The players reached the green of the eighteenth, and Sinn dropped in her putt for a birdie. Estill was three feet from the hole, putting for a birdie when play was stopped.

Estill and the Committee returned to the scene of her second shot, beneath the tree. The Committee asked the player to reenact her moves, and it was decided she had improved her area of intended swing, thus violating Rule 13-2—"A player shall not improve or allow to be improved the area of his intended swing." Violation of the Rule is loss of hole.

After this unfortunate situation, Sinn, who was soon to turn professional, commented, "I hope she knows how badly I feel about winning a match that way. I have lost matches before by not knowing the Rules of Golf. It's a terrible feeling and a miserable way to end an amateur career."

All of these situations, of course, create powerful arguments for staying out of the woods and avoiding trees at all costs—usually more easily said than done.

A variation on the Michelle Estill case occurred in September, 1986, during the twenty-fifth annual Luxembourg Open (an American tournament begun in 1962 by staff members of the *Stars and Stripes*). A player, whose name is lost in antiquity, struck his ball into the bountiful Luxembourgian woods but managed mercifully to find it. He took his stance and went into his backswing. His club struck a branch, and the club's shaft snapped off so that his downswing was executed with little more than his club grip.

Should he have been charged with a stroke, and possibly a penalty?

Unlike Estill, this player came away losing nothing for his trouble other than much of his club's shaft. He was not penalized, as his club broke on his backswing. A stroke is defined as the forward movement of the club made with the intention of fairly striking at and moving the ball. If a player checks his downswing voluntarily before the clubhead reaches the ball, he or she is deemed not to have made a stroke. In effect, this player had no club on his forward movement, thus under Decision 14/3 he took no stroke. If his club had broken on the downswing, he would have been charged with making a stroke.

That particular tournament, with its field of nearly sixty players, most of whom were above fifteen handicap and playing on a tight, testing course where some of the holes had the quality of hospital corridors, was memorable for its rulings (others appear elsewhere in this volume).

Prior to the Lux Open, a three-person Rules Committee was appointed. All were players in the tournament, so, as often as not, decisions were forthcoming on arguable issues only after all three—Mike Causey, Ben Abrams, and Bill Kelly—had finished their rounds and were unsafely sprawled in the clubhouse over a *Schos avec vodka,* annually the favored Luxembourg drink for smothering one's miseries.

Causey, who even called the USGA in Far Hills, New Jersey, from Luxembourg on one occasion (a six-hour time difference) for some legislative advice, remarked at tournament's end that in the future, "I'll work on the Rules Committee only if I'm paid by the hour." Abrams and Kelly agreed. Often they were forced to offer their decisions while surrounded by peevish players who would ask a question, then argue with the reply.

Much of the Northinch golf course in Perth, Scotland, makes it seem one is playing in a city park with fairways of limitless length. For that matter, the first and eighteenth holes at the Old Course in St. Andrews have that quality, with modifications at each, to the right sides. Superficially, this may seem equitable, a setting in which the less gifted player would never lose a golf ball nor face a recovery shot from woods or meadow.

106

More important, golf would also lose much of its remarkable character, developed out of the boundless possibilities of human beings contending with nature over control of that small, dimpled ball that commands the undivided attention of so many millions of otherwise rational beings.

VIII

TOOLS OF
THE TRADE

George, you look perfect . . .
that beautiful knitted shirt, an
alpaca sweater, those expensive
slacks . . . you've got an
alligator bag, the finest matched
irons, and the best woods money
can buy. It's a damned shame
you have to spoil it all by
playing golf.

—TOURING PRO
LLOYD MANGRUM,
TO COMEDIAN GEORGE BURNS

Golfers are a unique breed among practitioners of our individual participation sports—tennis, bowling, and golf are the conspicuous games—because they are tireless consumers, forever seeking the magic tool that will reduce their scores. An immense amount of money is spent each year in the United States on golf clubs, golf balls, shoes, and all the accoutrements, to say nothing about golf clothing. Turning these would-be athletes into well-attired butterflies is a major business in itself.

It isn't surprising that equipment plays a prominent role in the Rules of Golf—the section labeled "Clubs and the Ball" is second in the Rules book, appearing immediately after "The Game," and it has an appendix of its own in the back of the book.

This golfer enthusiasm for equipment hasn't been lost on the game's manufacturers, who are constantly stumping for the magical properties of their merchandise, which will guarantee straighter, longer shots, the ultimate sources of inner satisfaction to all players, especially if they can also putt.

111

Equipment questions have also supplied the greatest headaches for the game's governing bodies, because manufacturers are in a perpetual stir to refine their equipment, an activity almost guaranteeing changes that push clubs and balls, in particular, to or over the brink of acceptability. Upon any opposition or official resistance, the manufacturers unleash their battalions of barristers to sue the USGA, and/or the PGA, and/or the LPGA, and/or the Royal and Ancient. Our land is well stocked in attorneys on the lookout for a fast and large buck, so litigation has become as American as muggings.

Within the last twenty years, we've watched the brouhaha over a so-called "hot one," a lively ball that supposedly your Aunt Gladys would be able to smack over three hundred yards; the tiresome and currently resolved debate about the grooves of the Ping Eye2 irons that were developed by golf equipment manufacturer Karsten Solheim; and, most recently, the endless discussions about the long putter that seems most conspicuous on our increasingly popular Senior Tour.

Given the litigious, disputatious atmosphere around golf equipment, a bloated importance has befallen clubs, balls, and the incidentals. At the same time, equipment surfaces as a focal point of Rules and Decisions debates.

A new Decision, effective in 1991, was reached after an odd situation during the 1990 NCAA Golf Championships. Phil Mickelson, the defending champion, came to the first tee to begin his title defense, but first he counted his clubs routinely to make sure he had no more than the allowable fourteen. He had fourteen.

Sometime before Mickelson stepped up with his driver and hit his first shot, a teammate from Arizona State University with an identical golf bag returned from the practice green and mistakenly slipped his putter into Mickelson's bag. The champion noticed the extra club while playing the first hole, and immediately reported it. Under the Rules, a two-stroke penalty was in order.

Given the circumstances, it might seem the inadvertence would mitigate Mickelson's responsibility. He had counted his clubs once, and nothing was amiss. But no, the Decision was made by the USGA and Royal and Ancient; it was tough luck, Phil. In the official minds, he was responsible for what was in his bag upon the beginning of the round, and he

113

should have counted his clubs immediately before that first swing.

As it turned out, penalty or no, Mickelson safely defended his NCAA Championship, and he can be observed now carefully counting his clubs as a final, pre-tee shot action on the first tee.

Although clubs and balls are the chief equipment targets for Rules and Decisions governing golf, the modern electronic age has introduced some odd additions to equipment.

When a player brought along audio tapes and video tapes containing instructional material to assist him in his play, it prompted Jeff Bass, the golf professional at Canada Hills Country Club in Oro Valley, Arizona, to ask whether it was permissible, among other things, for a player's caddie to videotape the player's swing and replay it for him during the round?

No. It is a breach of Rule 14-3 to listen to audio tapes or view video tapes containing instructional or other information that might assist a player or, for that matter, any other electronic device containing such information. It seems likely that such devices could slow play and create something of a nightmare

114

on the course, giving it the character of the TV room at the local YMCA.

There's a neat irony to this: a *Golf Digest* magazine commercial on the ESPN cable network promoted an instructional tape that is being viewed by a player during his round on a portable TV on his golf cart. This is a clear violation of the Decision. Penalty for breach of 14-3, which disallows use of unusual artificial devices to aid a player, is severe: disqualification.

Shoes have even sidetracked a bit of the attention from clubs and golf balls. The spikeless golf shoes, which double nicely as an attractive and very comfortable dress shoe, are perfectly acceptable, but a type of inner wedge in a shoe that aids the player in assuming a correct stance is now under the critical eye of golf officials.

Historically, golf balls have undergone dramatic changes, beginning with the expensive *featherie* —a leather-bound ball that was stuffed manually with soaked, tightly packed goose feathers. It was surely an arduous chore, and these balls were much too costly for all but the most affluent. It is surprising that they were in use for more than four centuries. They were unreliable; often they assumed shapes

115

that would not guarantee predictable behavior, either in flight or when rolled along the ground.

When the ball made of gutta-percha, a Malayan elastic gum, showed up in 1848, the featherie was doomed, but its demise wasn't abrupt. The gutta-percha usually was softened in hot water, then rolled by hand on a flat board. When it became hard, it was able to weather the thrashings by clubs, and its spherical character allowed it to roll true. Yet being round and smooth, in the early stages of a round, the "gutties" would travel a short distance in the air, then plunge or dip. As it picked up nicks and scrapes, it behaved better, but the manufacturers of the featheries were snickering over these traits in the gutties.

Players routinely would reheat and reroll their gutties before rounds, and the same thing would happen. At last, it occurred to someone that a gutty flew better if it was battered and bruised, so it became the standard pre-round procedure to bang the ball with a hammer or some similar implement to roughen its surface, a precursor of dimples. It worked, and the featherie was finished.

Coburn Haskell, an American engineer from Cleveland, experimented with a rubber-core ball wrapped in elastic and wearing a gutta-percha cover,

116

and came up with a lively substitute for the unresponsive gutty. It reached Great Britain, and when Alexander Herd was introduced to the "Haskell" by amateur John Ball, he tried it, liked it, stocked up, and won the 1902 British Open.

This virtually guaranteed the death of the gutty.

The intervening years have seen gradual changes, although those dimples, a source of humor for many non-golfers, became a major element in the aeronautical scheme of golf-ball flight. Dimples helped the ball to remain airborne and curbed the smooth-ball tendency to swoon in mid-flight like some gunned-down creature.

It wasn't long before the dimple patterns varied, the number of dimples grew, and the shapes of the dimples changed from ball to ball. Each ball, of course, was touted by its manufacturer as the ultimate solution to all a player's numerous problems. One of the most popular themes has been the more dimples, the better. These dimplemongers were approaching four hundred to the ball at the most recent investigation. This may change, however, as hired engineers for competitors argue that larger, more shallow dimples are greater aids to the airborne golf ball.

Another variation among modern golf balls is the Cayman ball, manufactured deliberately to carry perhaps half as far as the standard golf ball. MacGregor Golf Company and Jack Nicklaus, who designed a course at Grand Cayman, in the Caribbean, with use of this ball in mind, are promoting the Cayman. It is a reasonable solution to an increasing problem within the game.

With a dramatic increase in the number of golfers, the need for more courses has accelerated even as good land for golf courses is in ever-decreasing supply and is frighteningly expensive. Smaller courses are one way around the nagging issue, and smaller courses demand a less lively ball.

So much for the evolution of the golf ball, whose modern changes are more numerous and subtle, lacking the impact of shifting from the featherie to the gutta-percha to the Haskell.

Golf ball approval has even reared its ugly head. Tom Watson showed up at a tournament and produced a Ram ball that wasn't included on the USGA list of conforming golf balls. It created a bit of a public relations problem, as Watson was acting as an advertising representative and was not allowed to use his company's ball.

Golf balls do creep into the Decisions; in fact, in a Decision that became effective on January 1, 1991, one of them fell into the hard-luck region with Mickelson's inadvertent fifteenth club. Here's what happened.

John Skaf, golf professional at the Coral Ridge Country Club in Fort Lauderdale, Florida, notified the USGA of the experience of a member at his club who, while playing a par-three hole, hit an excellent tee shot. But the ball struck the flagstick on the fly. To the player's astonishment, the impact caused the ball to break into two pieces. Two-thirds of the ball fell into the hole, and the remaining one-third came to rest close to the hole.

Surely, Skaf speculated, the player is credited with a hole in one, or, at worst, is left with an easy putt for a birdie.

No, and no. He must play again from the tee. This is dictated by Decision 5-3/4, based on the case of a ball shattering upon striking a paved cart path. The ball should be considered to have broken "as a result of a stroke," in which case the player must replay the stroke, but without penalty.

If golf balls underwent most of their alterations in the nineteenth and early twentieth centuries, golf

119

clubs have experienced their most dramatic changes in the last sixty years, beginning with the switch from wooden-shafted clubs to steel shafts. Since the steel shafts showed up in the early 1930s, other faddish innovations have made appearances, such as graphite shafts, but nothing has had the major consequence of the steel shafts.

It is almost too early to determine whether the metal woods have much real significance in the grand scheme of things. They seem to have officialdom's blessings—more than could be said of the narrowly spaced grooves that created such an irrational brouhaha in the late 1980s.

Even the much-discussed long putter has the qualified, perhaps temporary, approval of golf's governing bodies.

In a sense, the long putter arrived when it became the subject of a new Decision that was effective in 1990. The USGA received inquiries about the acceptability of using—even borrowing—a long putter to measure off relief under a Rule. The long putter is acceptable as a measuring device. Here was the formal question and its answer.

Q: A player, taking relief under a Rule, uses a driver to measure the one club-length or two club-lengths prescribed in the relevant Rule. He drops a ball correctly and the ball rolls less than two driver-lengths, but more than two putter-lengths, from where the ball first struck the ground when dropped.

Under Rule 20-2c, a dropped ball must be re-dropped if it rolls more than two club-lengths. If the ball comes to rest in a poor lie, may the player opt to use a putter to measure the distance the ball has rolled, in which case the player would re-drop under Rule 20-2c and escape the poor lie?

A: No. A player may use any club in measuring, including a club belonging to a partner, an opponent, or a fellow competitor, but the player must continue to use that club for all measuring required in the given situation.

The use of the long putter has come under some surveillance because manufacturers have been tinkering with it, fashioning a putter that essentially could be used at varying lengths. One of the problems with the long putter is that it may defy ready transportation on airline flights. As a result, manufacturers began to fiddle around with a shaft whose length could be reduced to a more transportable length. It soon became apparent that it might also be played at various lengths if the player felt this were beneficial.

This dilemma gave Frank Thomas, technical director of the USGA, something else to ponder as a string of putters poured into his office, their manufacturers seeking the blessing of the USGA.

Out of all this came the probability that beginning January 1, 1992, all putters would be limited to single grips—no more of these double-gripped putters that would allow gripping with the left hand (if the player were a right-hander) at a top grip, and with the right hand on a separate grip farther down the shaft.

In effect, the USGA would come to grips with grips. Ironically, one of the major users of the long putter was Orville Moody, the 1989 U.S. Senior Open Champion (a USGA Championship), who sadly predicted that his putter was doomed for rejection. To the contrary, it was given USGA blessings even though the grip modification was to be instituted at the beginning of 1992.

It should be suggested that if anyone thinks the last Rule or Decision has been levied about golf equipment, they would be well advised to think again. So long as manufacturers think they can sell more of their products by introducing innovations to them—the most common approach to distinguishing their tools from those of their competition—they will do so, and the USGA and the Royal and Ancient will remain busy yea- and nay-saying. It goes with the territory.

IX

HELP THE HANDICAPPED

*Nothing goes down slower than a
golf handicap.*

—BOBBY NICHOLS,
Never Say Never, 1965

Perhaps no game played by human beings consumes more hours to calculate methods of equalizing competition between players than golf. The business of handicapping is conducted most avidly at the lower end of the scale, for the golfers of more modest talents. It is logical, of course; they need all the help possible.

Although many amateur golfers are accustomed to playing weekly with the same handful of friends, working out their skill differences based on their knowledge of each other's abilities, so that Bill gives Harry three strokes a side by common consent, highly formalized handicapping also exists. Indeed, it has reached such a level of sophistication that under the odd label of Slope System—*Slope* derives from the angled line formed on a sheet of graph paper where all the pertinent information is recorded— decimal points are used to register fractional differences. The whole exercise is a mathematician's dream.

Teams of golfers armed with clipboards actually walk golf courses to estimate their comparative ease or difficulty, eventually assigning a rating to each course so that it can be measured against other courses.

Briefly, that means that if you develop your handicap at an easy course, you'll receive additional strokes when you play a tougher course. If, on the other hand, you built your handicap at a tough golf course, you'll lose strokes when you wander onto a more simple spread.

The underlying philosophy of all this is to create equity among players of contrasting abilities, thus, in theory at least, increasing the pleasure for everyone. With the correct handicap, you should be a match for Greg Norman or Nick Faldo or Betsy King or Tom Kite.

Golf is not alone in its vigorous efforts to build in an equalizer. Bowling has something similar, a handicap based on a percentage difference between a player's average game and an arbitrary score of 200. In horseracing, which gave us the term *handicap* in the first place (literally, "hand in cap," as bettors wagered on a race's outcome, picking an entry's name from a hat), horses were weighted in an attempt to equalize the field.

Golf's elaborate handicap system is, in truth, the product of more than a century of calculations, beginning among the women players of Great Britain in the late nineteenth century.

One might think that given all the years of thought and figuring going into the modern golf handicap system, questions or disputes would be minimal. Certainly the geniuses who have spent so many hours of brain time to devise this near-perfect balance among players would have missed nothing in their eager pursuit of a flawless handicap system

Think again.

The human capacity to find ridges and rifts in the most adroitly conceived scheme is enormous.

For example, a pair of handicap Rules inspired this letter from Mrs. C. L. Graham of Long Lake, Minnesota who asked:

How strictly should Rules 37-6 and 37-7 (re: discontinuance of play and undue delay) be applied in recording scores for handicap purposes? It is not unusual for some players to play nine holes, take time out for lunch, and then play the last nine holes. Should scores so made be recorded for handicap purposes, or should they be omitted from the handicap records as not being part of an eighteen-hole round?

On the face of it, the issue seems innocent and almost frivolous. Stopping for lunch? So what else is new? But read on. Here's the answer:

Taking time out for lunch between the playing of the first and last nine holes constitutes a violation of Rule 37-6a for which the penalty is disqualification. However, to eliminate such scores from players' scoring records might mean loss of a considerable number of scores, which undoubtedly contribute to a better picture of their playing ability. Accordingly, we recommend that such scores be accepted for *handicap purposes only.*

This reply came from John P. English, who was assistant executive director for the Handicap Procedure Committee.

Even the character of a golf course has been brought into question. A player asked, "May USGA Handicaps be computed from scores made on par-three courses if the par-three courses have been rated in accordance with the USGA Course Rating System?"

The response wasn't terribly surprising.

No. Scores are not acceptable for USGA Handicaps when made on par-three courses or other courses where the majority of holes are not par fours and fives.. Such courses do not normally place a premium on distance or variety of strokes, factors which are important in play on standard courses; hence, it would not be equitable to handicap players on such short courses on the same basis as players on standard courses. A par-three course does not normally require the use of a full set of clubs. A score on such a course is analogous to a score made in a competition in which the types of clubs are limited; such scores are prohibited in USGA Handicap computations by Section 4-4b. However, scores made on par-three and similar courses may be used with the USGA Handicap and Course Rating Systems to produce equitable handicaps for use at such courses only. Handicaps so produced may not be termed "USGA Handicaps." USGA Handicaps produced by scores at other courses may be used fairly at short courses if no other types of handicap are permitted.

Author of this response was the late P. J. Boatwright. He also ruled on abuse that surfaced in Phoenix, Arizona. Here was the complaint:

There is quite a problem here in Phoenix concerning a few women who regularly, when playing poorly, walk off the course after fifteen or sixteen holes. They do not wish their handicaps to increase and therefore eliminate them from their club's teams. This has become quite an issue and I have been asked to get the USGA's comments.

The letter from Mrs. Edgar B. Pease evoked this reply from Boatwright:

Section 4-1 and 4-4 of the USGA Golf Handicap System provide that scores made when less than an eighteen-hole round is played may not be entered in any form in the player's handicap record. However, it is not intended that this provision be used by players to prevent use of scores that would affect their handicaps.

The USGA Golf Handicap System, like the Rules of Golf, assumes that players will be honest. The Handicap Committee would be justified in withdrawing the handicap of a player who abuses a provision of the system.

Behind the scenes, the question of honesty is often cropping up, and for the silliest of reasons. One player in the group with whom I played regularly during our days with the *Stars and Stripes* newspaper in West Germany had the habit of going out to Frankfurt or Heidelberg after work and playing a round alone. In summer, it remained light late enough to play until after nine o'clock in the evening.

This fellow, who was our best player beyond question, would play extra balls. If he hit a bad shot, he'd do it again to get it right. He held up no one; he was alone and he invariably was in mid-fairway and reasonably long.

He would not record those scores. Predictably, a few players would grumble at the Press Club, pointing out that he carried a low handicap yet showed only a dozen or so scores. The exact character of their complaints was hard to understand; clearly; he was not sandbagging—that is, recording scores higher than his ability, and he was merely doing on a fairly empty golf course what others might do at the driving range.

The real reason for their complaints probably came down to this: he beat them regularly.

But was he behaving correctly in not recording his scores? A quarter-century ago, the issue was raised—and answered by the USGA. The question was, "When a golfer plays a practice round or a round alone, does he have to turn in the score for handicap purposes? If so, is there any limit on how many such scores a player may return?"

The answer left little doubt.

If by "practice round" you mean a round in which the player plays practice shots from hazards, plays more than one ball in the round or otherwise does not play in accordance with the Rules, the score made *should not be used* in handicap computations.

If, on the other hand, a "practice round" is a round played in accordance with the Rules, it should be used in computations.

Playing a "practice round" alone does not eliminate the score from handicap computations, provided the player has endeavored to make the best score he can at each hole in the eighteen-hole round. Scores need not be attested. There is no limit on how many scores made while playing alone may be used.

Handicaps would not seem normally to attract the bizarre turns or twists of incident, but even here novelty makes its appearance.

What happens when a left-handed player decides to switch over to right-handed?

"A member of our association recently changed from left-handed to right-handed play," wrote a woman from San Antonio, Texas. "She has a handicap based on scores made playing left-handed, but because she considers this a whole new game for her, she would like to start over and establish a new handicap playing right-handed. The new handicap would be issued when she has returned five right-handed scores. Is this permissible or must her left-handed scores continue to be used on a decreasing basis until she has returned twenty right-handed scores?"

This inquiry should give some indication of the types of issues that pepper the mail and the telephone calls at USGA headquarters. Whatever else it may be, it is seldom dull.

The answer: "The player in question is, in effect, beginning golf anew and thus she should be required to establish a new handicap based solely on scores made playing right-handed. The new handicap would not be valid if subsequently the player changed her mind and began playing left-handed again."

A modern sociological—and geographical—trend even imposes itself on the handicap scene.

People are living longer, and it is increasingly common for mature couples to retire to the Sunbelt of America—roughly from the Carolinas across the southern boundary of our continent to New Mexico, Arizona, and southern California. And yes, they take up golf, a game sufficiently peaceful to be played by our elders without a serious threat to their health.

What happens, however, is this: husband and wife compete on the golf course, and suddenly the tranquillity disappears in disputes over their handicaps‚because of course ratings from the forward and the middle tees.

It wasn't a Sunbelt dispute (Minnesota is at some remove from the likes of Arizona), but this debate became public in early 1987, and it was a good example of what can happen.

The contentiousness centered on Section 8-4f of the Handicap Manual. Mrs. Clara Bleak, of Bloomington, Minnesota, wrote to praise the USGA on its efforts to improve the Handicap System, and she added that she was pleased that she and her husband now could play from the same tees.

136

However . . .

It never fails. The eternal burr in the perpetual blanket. Mrs. Bleak thought it ironic that she and her husband could shoot the same scores, yet she would give him strokes because the course was rated as tougher for women from the "men's tees" (her term, now desexed to "middle tees").

Her reasoning: the course rating for women at her club is 66.7, while it is 62.5 for men. If she and her husband played the middle tees exclusively, and both shot 85s, her course rating of 66.7 would produce a differential of 18.3 against her husband's 22.5 (85 minus 62.5). Therefore, she would give him strokes.

No, no, no. Section 8-4f reads: "When players competing against one another are playing from different sets of tees, the player playing from the set of tees from which the Course Rating is higher shall receive additional handicap strokes equal to the difference between the two Course Ratings. *The same applies if a man and woman compete from the same set of tees.*" The italics are ours.

Decimals are rounded off to the nearest whole number, with a decimal of five being rounded upward. Example: If a woman playing from the forward, or red tees, from which the Women's Course Rating is 73.5, competes against a man playing from the middle tees, from which the Men's Course Rating is 70.9, the woman shall add three strokes $(73.5 - 70.9 = 2.6$, rounded upward) to her course handicap.

What was the impact of this convoluted issue? Here are a few bits from Mrs. Bleak's final letter:

> I really appreciate what you're trying to do to help me. Unfortunately, my husband is not convinced that I should have strokes added to my handicap because the course rating is not the same for both of us. He believes that if the Rating/Slope Systems work as they are intended, no other adjustment is necessary. I don't think there is any way to convince him otherwise.
>
> Thanks to you, though, we have been able to work out a compromise that should keep peace in the family. He's agreed to let me use a handicap based on his Course Rating, so if we're shooting the same scores we'll have the same handicap. Needless to say, that will apply only to the games between the two of us. If the end result is the same as if I added the

138

extra strokes to my legitimate handicap—I suspect it may turn out to be close—then maybe he'll be convinced.

It is tough to decide what is most impressive about this entire 8-4f exercise; its mathematical complexity, or the debate evoked by the issue. It could test a shaky marriage.

Upon completing this chapter, we decided to brighten the day for Director Dean Knuth and his gang in the Handicap Department by posing this question: A player from Long Island, New York, is a member of a club that closes up shop in the winter—that is, no golf, no handicap chairman, etc. Our player, who carries a nine handicap, goes to Florida and shoots ten successive 75s on a par-seventy course, which should qualify him for about a four handicap. Moreover, he is invited down to play in a member/guest tournament in Jacksonville in February.

Should he play off the nine handicap he had when the handicap chairman packed it in for the winter, or should he elicit a second opinion? The reply has now come down from the handicap oracles: he must await the return of spring and his club's handicap chairman.

X

THINGS THAT DEFY PIGEONHOLING

If you watch a game, it's fun. If you play it, it's recreation. If you work at it, it's golf.

—BOB HOPE,
Reader's Digest, 1958

141

Within golf, many things happen that do not fall neatly into sharply defined categories. Dr. Richard Silver, a retired New York City dentist who loves the Rules of Golf, enjoys telling the illustrative story of a young man who was attempting to qualify for an amateur tournament in the East. Dr. Silver was officiating at the time. (Alluding to his role as an official, Dr. Silver mentions the heart transplant candidate who was offered a choice among hearts that had belonged to an Olympic athlete, a reformed alcoholic, and a golf official. He opted for the golf official's heart: "It has never been used.")

His aside out of the way, Dr. Silver returned to the young player seeking to qualify for match play. He hit a long drive far to the right, in the deep grass of the rough. His caddie was optimistic, so they headed in the direction of his shot. After searching for a couple of minutes without success, it was decided the caddie would continue the search while the player returned to hit another tee shot. This one was down the middle, albeit a bit short of his first ball.

The player went to his second ball and was about to hit it toward the green when the caddie called to him, saying he had found the player's first shot. The player picked up his second ball, and returned to the rough. He dug the ball out of the thick grass, but left his shot well short of the green.

To his consternation, the player discovered upon reaching the ball that it wasn't his. He had hit the wrong ball. Dr. Silver was standing near, and he quickly saw the young man's distress. Silver wanted to commiserate, but in truth, the lad had accumulated a batch of shots.

In the first place, when he returned to hit a second tee shot, he was hitting three. When he erroneously picked up his second ball, that cost him a one-stroke penalty and the ball must be replaced. He incurred another two for hitting the wrong ball. Now he's looking at his seventh shot, and he must replace his ball on the fairway where he picked up his second ball.

Faced with his own unhappiness and a traffic jam piling up behind him, the young man gestured to his caddie and, walking beside Dr. Silver, called a halt to his round, saying only, "I have to learn the Rules of this game."

Occasionally, an incident will occur that is grounds for pause even among the experts. A Virginia woman who happens to be a friend of Tom Meeks, the director of Rules and Competitions for the USGA, told him about a novel incident during the Virginia Women's Amateur Championship a few years ago.

A good player was playing the par-five seventeenth hole and after two good shots was left with a short wedge over a pond to the waiting green. As she approached the pond, she noticed two men in a small rowboat on the pond. They were removing a choking infestation of water hyacinth; the men were oblivious to the tournament passing them by. But not for long.

The player's planned lofty wedge shot turned into a line drive, and it headed directly toward the two men in the boat. There wasn't time for them to row to safety. The ball struck an inside wall of the craft, ricocheted around, striking an ankle or calf in its flight before coming to rest at the bottom of the rowboat.

She called her apologies, but they just laughed. No one was hurt. One of the men tossed the ball back to her. She dropped it a few feet from the water, hit what she counted as her fifth shot, and finished the hole with seven.

Later, during a casual discussion at USGA headquarters, Meeks and P. J. Boatwright Jr., suggested that if the two men had agreed—and it seemed likely they would have—she could have ridden out in the boat to the point where it was parked when her ball struck it and shot for the green from the boat without penalty. In effect, it was no different than a bridge over the water. She would have been hitting four from the rowboat.

At worst, she might have done this and dropped one as she did, and let the Committee thrash it out (and call the USGA) upon completion of her round.

So, yes, it is useful to know a bit about the Rules and their Decisions if golf is to be played successfully beyond the casual weekend level.

Sometimes it isn't even enough to know the Rules and Decisions, because they are subject to change. In the 1985 U.S. Women's Open, at the Baltusrol Golf Club's Upper Course in Springfield, New Jersey, Jan Stephenson marked and lifted her ball on a green and tapped down the marker on the dewy grass with the bottom of her putter.

Unnoticed immediately by her, the marker adhered to her putter, so when she discovered it, she was unsure where her ball lay. She knew it wasn't on the bottom of her putter, where the marker was sticking.

At the time, she was assessed a stroke penalty for having moved her ball (without properly marking it). But, ah! That has been changed, rendered more forgiving. The USGA and Royal and Ancient experts decided the penalty was inappropriate in that incident, and, upon revision, she would have been permitted to replace her ball at a point as near as possible to where she and her opponent agreed it lay, but no nearer the hole, no penalty.

This should not be muddled, however, with a situation in which the ball marker has stuck to the bottom of one's golf shoe. Here's what happened, resulting in a Decision that was effective beginning January 1, 1990.

A player marked the position of his ball on the putting green and lifted the ball. When it was the player's turn, he could not find his ball marker. Subsequently, he found it adhering to the sole of his shoe. He concluded that he had accidentally stepped on it while assisting his partner in lining up a putt.

147

Tough luck. The player incurred a penalty stroke under Rule 20-1, which requires that the position of a ball be marked before it is lifted and contemplates that the ball marker will remain in position until the ball is replaced. The player must place the ball as near as possible to its original position but not nearer the hole—Rule 20-3c.

Under the final paragraph of Rule 20-1, a player is exempt from penalty if the ball marker is accidentally moved in the process of lifting the ball or marking its position (the Jan Stephenson case). In this case, the ball marker was not moved during such a process.

Quite apart from Chi Chi Rodriguez's whimsical observation that he began his golf career in Puerto Rico as a ball marker, marking one's golf ball has produced some anguished moments in the game. For example, in the 1983 U.S. Amateur Public Links Championship, played at Hominy Hill in Colt's Neck, New Jersey, Billy Tuten defeated David Hobby, 3 and 1, but not before the match was leveled on the thirteenth hole when Tuten failed to return his ball to its original position on the green after marking it off the line of a Hobby putt.

Oddly enough, it was a member of the gallery who pointed out Tuten's oversight as he, Hobby, and the crowd walked to the fourteenth hole. It would happen again in this same championship. Playing for a spot in the quarterfinals, Tom Piscopink and Charles Nieman were even after eighteen holes. On the first extra hole, Piscopink marked his ball off Nieman's line. When Piscopink lined up his putt, he failed to return it to its original point, and Nieman quickly warned him, a sportsmanlike gesture. Piscopink won the match on the twentieth hole, when he could have lost were it not for Nieman's quick admonition.

For contrast to sportsmanship, during the Massachusetts Open, Andrew Morse, an amateur, had a one-stroke victory all but assured on the final green, where he marked his ball off the putting line of a professional player who was tied for second with another professional. They, of course, were playing for money prizes.

The player holed the putt, and Morse, smelling victory, placed his ball by his marker and rolled in his putt for an apparent victory. But no— the professional pointed out to Morse that he had failed to return his ball to its original place. The oversight cost Morse two strokes, and the championship. Clearly, the professional knew enough that he could have warned Morse; he chose not to, which may say volumes about that player's character.

Something about golf seems to lure the absurd incident, and a classic instance occurred in Luxembourg, when an American tournament in 1986 seemed to be generously sprinkled with unlikely happenings.

Among the more novel in that outing was the playing of the wrong hole, and under the most conspicuous of circumstances. For those unacquainted with the Luxembourg course, coming off the par-three seventeenth hole can be confusing because the ninth tee area headed toward the clubhouse visible in the middle distance is much closer than the eighteenth tee area, which you reach by walking through heavy woods behind and to the right of the seventeenth green.

A sizable gang of players were sitting on the clubhouse terrace in the sunshine with their drinks when they noticed three players clearly playing their approach shots to the ninth green. The reactions on the terrace ranged from "Did it take them that long to reach the ninth hole?" to "They were right behind us at the fifteenth hole."

It wasn't complicated; they were playing the wrong hole. After hurried consultation and a few shouts, the group on the terrace got the attention of the misguided trio, who returned some five hundred yards to the eighteenth tee and completed their first rounds on the correct hole. What was the correct procedure and penalty, if any? Each of the three wayfarers sustained two penalty strokes for teeing off from outside the correct teeing grounds in a stroke-play tournament (Rule 11-4b).

Even putting gets into the act. During that same Decisions-laden tournament, an exasperated player missed a short putt on the eighteenth green—again, in front of a large gallery—and reaching over, tapped the still-rolling ball into the hole. Two of the three members of the Rules Committee witnessed this gaffe. The decision was swift and unanimous: the player was penalized two strokes for striking a ball in motion.

Also in the putting category, a competitor about to putt inadvertently struck his ball with a practice swing prior to actually addressing the ball. Should he be charged with a stroke and forced to play the ball from its new position?

This incident inspired the liveliest debate. The Committee allowed the player to replace his ball without penalty. However, Rule 18-2a(ii), augmented by Decision 18-2a/20, requires that if the competitor causes the ball to move, the competitor shall incur a penalty stroke and the ball must be replaced; if it is not replaced, the competitor incurs a total penalty of two strokes. So, the Committee erred, although its decision stands.

This was the incident that inspired the call to the USGA from Luxembourg, and a faint, flickering light was shed across an ocean as well as the thousands of miles, a distant candle in the murky darkness of a Rules Committee's typical day.

There's little question that bizarre Decisions are going to surface every year, notwithstanding the disbelief expressed by Bud Semple, late president of the USGA Executive Committee, two decades ago when he was chairman of the Rules of Golf Committee. He found it incredible that new Decisions situations continued to arise year after year. He thought that all of the unusual situations possible should have occurred and been dealt with by then. As Boatwright succinctly responded to that sentiment, "No such luck."

To support Boatwright's position—twenty-three new Decisions came into existence effective January 1, 1991, and many of them fall into the ambiguous category of those that defy pigeonholing.

AFTERWORD: MEANWHILE, BACK AT THE GOLF COURSE . . . .

There are now more golf clubs in the world than Gideon Bibles, more golf balls than missionaries and, if every golfer in the world, male and female, were laid end to end, I for one would leave them there.

—MICHAEL PARKINSON, PRESIDENT, ANTI-GOLF SOCIETY

The notion that there's nothing new under the sun may be true in some areas of human experience, but Decisions governing golf is not one of them. I'm not at all sure that the Rules are immutable, for that matter. After all, they did grow from thirteen originally to the current thirty-four. Who is to say that eager legislators won't create new Rules, perhaps as personal monuments to themselves, at some future time. It is a trait endemic to the human condition.

When a game is played out of doors, as we've seen, diversity among the things that can happen is seemingly infinite. Given its terrain, foliage, animal life, and exposure to a variety of elements, the golf course can't be likened to a meeting room in a motel or to a tennis court or any other playground for sportive types.

The average area covered by a golf course is 160 acres (this is variable, from the 120 acres that manage to accommodate the great Open course of Merion, in Ardmore, Pennsylvania, outside Philadelphia, to the Eagle Creek public course in Indianapolis, sprawling over 325 acres). The character of any golf acreage may range from desert tundra to oceanside linksland to rolling meadowlike property to heavily wooded territory. In the course of a golf career, a player may encounter beasts of all sizes, shapes, and temperaments, be forced into difficult decisions involving trees, penalty options, hazards of one sort or another, and disasters of one's own making.

As already shown, even the innocuous subject of the handicaps—which perhaps generates more interest and attention among golfers contacting the USGA than any other single topic—takes on the character of a major issue.

For example, a quarterfinal match was played at the Heidelberg military golf course in what was then West Germany in the annual Stars and Stripes Golf Association Championship. The adversaries were Denny Harrell and Marianne Schuettler.

The fifth hole at Heidelberg at the time was a par-four for men and rated their toughest hole, while it was a par-five for women and rated the course's twelfth most difficult for them. This was in the 1970s, thus predating the whole business of Slope;

moreover, these military courses in Europe weren't rated, so par served as the basis for handicaps.

Here was the rub—since Schuettler's handicap was twenty-six and Harrell's twelve, he received a stroke on the hole against his par-four, while she at twenty-six would receive one stroke against a par-five ranked as the twelfth most difficult. They both scored fives—for her, a par and a net four, for him a bogey and also a net four. Who won the hole?

She lost the match to him, one up. It was deemed they had halved the fifth hole with matching fives, a decision I still question—I think her par should beat his bogey—and the argument over the situation raged during a long, freezing German winter.

That is why each year new Decisions are published to shed further light (or create more murkiness) on a game whose legislative literature already seems endless. Certainly, the end isn't in sight, as this book attests.

Arguably, we may be grateful for this: Certainly, clubhouse conversations are richer for the debates that are inspired by such occurrences, and perhaps only baseball enjoys a sense of its own history to match that of golf.

As we've seen, the range of circumstances is all but interminable. There's a what-next? quality to this game just when you may think you've seen it all.

So, anyone who promotes and entertains the illusion that there's nothing new under the sun clearly has never played golf.

To illustrate: a recent letter to the USGA from a California golfer asked whether removal of a dead elk from a player's shot path was permissible on the fairway. The man had enlisted the help of his playing partner to haul the beast out of the way, and had aroused the skepticism and annoyance of their opponents in a match, but he was within his rights.

The elk, being dead, was loose impediment; thus, being on the fairway and not in a hazard, the unfortunate brute was movable.

Yes, indeed—there *are* things new under the sun, and so shall it ever be where golf is concerned.